Cecelia

64-

fresno CA.

8.20. 2011

Boo

twins ✳✳✳✳✳
✳✳✳✳✳

6271
806. 559,
559, 579
2148

GET UP,,
GET OUT,
GET BLESSED!

B R Y A N CUTSHALL

GET UP,
GET OUT,
GET BLESSED

Delivered from Bondage, Through the Wilderness,
and into Your Promised Land

WHITAKER
HOUSE

Unless otherwise indicated, Scripture quotations are taken from the *New King James Version*, © 1979, 1980, 1982, 1984 by Thomas Nelson, Inc. Used by permission. All rights reserved. Scripture quotations marked (NIV) are from the Holy Bible, *New International Version*®, NIV®, © 1973, 1978, 1984 by the International Bible Society. Used by permission of Zondervan. All rights reserved. Scripture quotations marked (KJV) are taken from the King James Version of the Holy Bible.

Some definitions of words are taken from *Merriam-Webster's 11ᵗʰ Collegiate Dictionary*. Hebrew definitions are taken from *Strong's Hebrew Dictionary*.

GET UP, GET OUT, GET BLESSED:
Delivered from Bondage, through the Wilderness, and into Your Promised Land

Bryan Cutshall Ministries
10575 Tesson Ferry Rd.
St. Louis, MO 63123
www.churchtrainer.com

ISBN: 978-1-60374-054-8
Printed in the United States of America
© 2008 by Bryan Cutshall

Whitaker House
1030 Hunt Valley Circle
New Kensington, PA 15068
www.whitakerhouse.com

Library of Congress Cataloging-in-Publication Data

Cutshall, Bryan.
Get up, get out, get blessed : delivered from bondage, through the wilderness, and into your promised land / by Bryan Cutshall.
p.   cm.
Summary: "Applies the Israelites' journey out of Egypt, through the wilderness, and into the Promised Land of Canaan to a Christian's spiritual life in leaving the things of the world behind"—Provided by publisher.
ISBN 978-1-60374-054-8 (trade pbk. : alk. paper) 1. Exodus, The.
2. Christian life—Biblical teaching. I. Title.
BS1199.E93C88 2008
248.4—dc22   2008012130

No part of this book may be reproduced or transmitted in any form or by any means, electronic or mechanical—including photocopying, recording, or by any information storage and retrieval system—without permission in writing from the publisher. Please direct your inquiries to permissionseditor@whitakerhouse.com.

1 2 3 4 5 6 7 8 9 10 11 12 ʊʃ 16 15 14 13 12 11 10 09 08

FOREWORD

T his is a book worth reading! Bryan Cutshall is a successful young pastor who shows in this new book why the Old
Testament can be such a powerful tool in coping with the
problems of twenty-first-century living. He uses the path of the
Hebrew children, getting out of Egypt, through the wilderness, and
into the Promised Land, as a metaphor for life in modern times
for all Christians. And he does it with clarity, simplicity, and great
effectiveness.

If read simply as a retelling of the Old Testament narrative of
Israel's flight from captivity, this book is worthwhile. It brings that
familiar biblical account to life in a fresh way. Beyond a mere retelling of a familiar Bible story, however, is Cutshall's gift for making
applications that are helpful to modern believers. In his book, Cutshall shows a love and understanding for the Old Testament, and
an unusual ability to use Old Testament stories to illuminate and
comment on contemporary issues.

Cutshall is not primarily an Old Testament theological scholar
but a pastor—and it shows. His pastoral eye for the application of
principles is the strongest aspect of his writing. In every chapter, he
weaves the experiences of his pastoral ministry into the story of the
Hebrew refugees, and with wonderful effect.

The pattern Cutshall follows is a simple one: getting out of
Egypt, getting through the Wilderness, entering the Promised Land,

and conquering Canaan is the challenge everyone faces in every generation. There are memorable lessons in this book for every reader, whether a veteran traveler on the Christian path, or a newcomer to it. I recommend *Get Up, Get Out, Get Blessed* with enthusiasm.

—Charles Paul Conn
President, Lee University
Cleveland, Ohio

CONTENTS

PART III: The Promised Land and How to Get In

PART IV: Conquering Canaan

Introduction

Where are the champions—the present-day heroes of the Christian faith? Where are those who walk and talk what they claim they would die for? Where are those who would stand up to the naysayers and become "yea-sayers"? It takes such little effort to be average, and almost no effort to be mediocre. Has the average, the status quo, become the accepted Christian norm of the day?

Victory is still possible for those who are willing to climb mountains, walk through deserts, and hold on to divine promises. Our goal is not to simply make it to heaven or to barely avoid hell. We have been promised quality of life—Canaan land! This promise is not a figment of hopeful imagination; it is a tangible reality for pilgrims who are willing to finish the journey. There are no shortcuts or quick-fix remedies. Ridding ourselves of carnality is a tough walk up the less-traveled road called "paying the price"—the only route to the winner's circle. Codependent.

The Christian life is not merely existing until Christ comes back for His church. Rather, the Christian life is

- a battleground for not only fighting giants, but also killing giants.
- a pathway for not only walking through valleys, but also walking out of valleys.

9

- a place of trust where you not only live by faith, but also live in faith.

- a passageway of learning to focus your life, yoke with Christ, and align with the road map of God's Word.

- a proclamation of a lifestyle of destiny and divine promise.

Leave the drudgeries behind; sound the trumpet of war to Satan's forces, declaring your determination to join the land of the living. Leave a legacy of victory behind for those who dare to pursue the tracks of the determined. *Get Up, Get Out, Get Blessed*—by a life filled with exploits of excellence.

With these convictions I write this book, which not only identifies the struggles within, but also sheds light on the less-traveled trail leading to Canaan. Come join the pilgrimage of the Israelites. Identify with their struggles. Learn from their mistakes. Feast on their manna, and prepare for a new way of living—living on His promises.

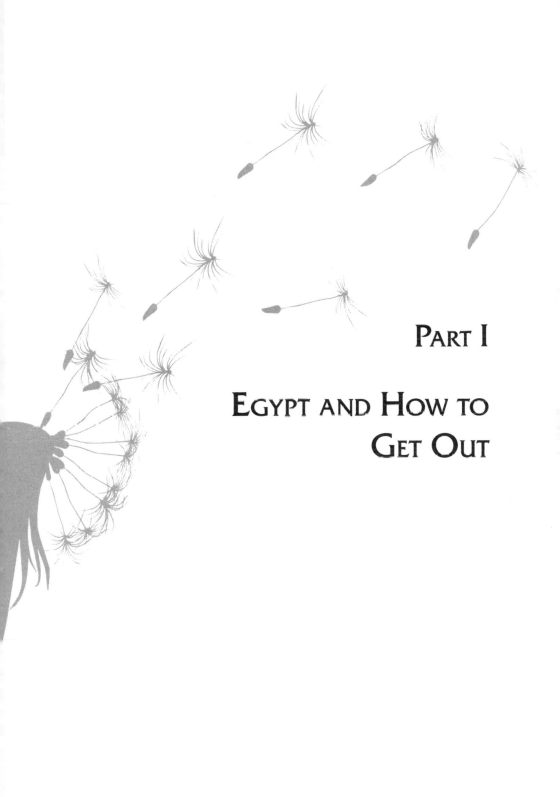

PART I

EGYPT AND HOW TO GET OUT

chapter 1

HOW DID EGYPT GET INTO ME?

CAMPING AT HARAN

Flashbulbs popped all around the room, creating a strobe effect. The woman behind the microphone squinted and shielded her eyes. "You keep flashing, making it hard for me to read your lips. Can you hold it for a minute?" she asked.

The news conference was the first of many for Heather Whitestone, the newly crowned Miss America who had become deaf at the age of eleven. The twenty-one-year-old junior from Jacksonville State University had only 5 percent hearing in her left ear. Heather read lips, however, wore a large hearing aid, and used sign language to compensate for her hearing loss.

Heather's character reflected her philosophy. She did not view her disability as a handicap. Rather, she believed, "The most handicapped person in the world is a negative thinker." Heather told the audience that, when she was a child, her mother often told her that the last four letters of *American* is "I-C-A-N."

Heather proceeded to tour the United States on a grueling speaking circuit, declaring to young people with and without disabilities that "anything is possible!"

During the talent portion of the pageant, Heather had performed a ballet routine that had brought the audience to tears as she danced to the music, "Via Dolorosa." She was able to dance by feeling the vibrations of the music, counting the beats in her head, and synchronizing her dance movements to reflect the changes in pitch.

What motivated Heather to accomplish such stunning achievements? Was it a special advantage or privilege that she had over others in life? Was it money, pedigree, or influence that brokered her success? Maybe it was extraordinary talent or intellect that did it.

No, in spite of the handicaps, hardships, and heartbreaks, Heather Whitestone achieved the impossible because of her belief that she could overcome any problem that threatened to keep her from achieving her goals. Heather's formula for success is simple. Anyone who chooses to use it can attain high levels of accomplishment—even the impossible. Her formula is this:

1. Believe you are who God says you are.
2. Believe anything is possible.

DESTINED FOR GREATNESS

Deep in the soul of mankind are seeds of success—seeds sown by God when He created mankind. This is why men and women compete against each other and strive to be the very best they can be.

God is whole and complete. When man was created by God, he received the reflection (in measure) of God's nature. Humanity's prototype was made complete in every way, fitted to win.

The image of mankind's Maker reflects upon our souls and upon our dreams for success and victory.

Down but Not Out

When Mount St. Helens belched forth fire and brimstone, tens of thousands of square miles of Eden-like landscape were suddenly transformed into a hellish moonscape unfit for habitation. Life was instantly extinguished. The crisp scent of springtime changed into the acrid stench of death and destruction that will last for decades to come.

Similarly, when Adam fell, he was totally corrupted. The image of God, once aglow in man's heart, flickered. God's image in man's heart became polluted with selfishness, greed, and sin. The precious seeds God had planted in mankind were exposed and contaminated by the consequences of mankind's spiritual fall. The damage was total and complete.

> *Deep in the soul of mankind are seeds of success— seeds sown by God when He created mankind.*

So it is with fallen man today. He reflects the distorted image he carries of his Creator. His values, goals, dreams, emotions, and physical well-being have all been affected. What once was a clear reflection of God's image is now marred and corrupted.

Man's fallout was far-reaching—more so than the debacle at the Chernobyl nuclear power station in the Ukraine. When that protective superstructure was breached, it released billows of radioactive chemicals into the atmosphere, infecting thousands with sickness and death.

The fallout of Eden does not discriminate. It takes its toll on men, women, and children for generations.

TWO THREADS

A powerful analogy of how fallen creation influences and affects everything within it is found in the Old Testament book of Genesis. Of the many historical accounts, revelations, and relationships described in this book, two threads run throughout its pages. One is the golden thread of achievement and freedom; the other is the black thread of failure and bondage.

The golden thread of achievement begins with the promise of God.

THE PROMISE

Mankind started down the long spiral of disobedience, trapped in an endless cycle of failure. The forces of a fallen nature were pulling him faster toward destruction. He repeated the same mistakes as he tried, without success, to break this cycle of misery and mediocrity.

Until, one day, God planted in the heart of a man a noble seed of His promises, which ultimately led mankind back to Him. This journey of faith began as an excursion of trust, with God's promises as the sole road map. The pathway of promise began with a pilgrim named Abram. We pick up his story and the beginning of his journey in Genesis 12:1–4.

> *Now the LORD had said to Abram: "Get out of your country, from your family and from your father's house, to a land that I will show you. I will make you a great nation; I will bless you and make your name great; and you shall be a blessing. I will bless those who bless you, and I will curse him who curses you; and in you all the families of the earth shall be blessed." So Abram departed as the LORD had spoken to him.*
>
> (Genesis 12:1–4)

God selected Abram to break through the atmosphere of evil and debauchery that sin had bred. Abram, probably much like anyone today, was not a superman. Moreover, his society was in turmoil and everyone was doing his or her own thing.

Suddenly, life as Abram knew it changed. God promised him amazing things during his lifetime—achievements that would impact the entire human race for all time. God Himself guaranteed the fulfillment of these promises:

1. Abram would father a great nation of people.
2. He would have God's blessing rest upon him and upon his descendents.
3. He would be a blessing to the nations of the world.

God planted in Abram's heart the seed of His promises. Now it became Abram's responsibility to obey. However, the "fallout" of a fallen nature affected Abram and, as we shall see, he constantly fought a battle against the pull of the world trying to reclaim him. *promises*

Abram was living at his father's house. Archaeological evidence shows that those who lived in Ur worshipped the moon god, Sin. Before God could fulfill His divine plan in Abram's life, He had to get Abram away from Sin and get the influence of Sin out of Abram.

HARAN—THE CROSSROADS

Soon, Abram was off with a band of travelers following the dream of a better life—a promise God told him would be fulfilled in a land called Canaan. This became Abram's destination. However, many delays and detours occurred because of the pull of family and friends *husbands who are not husbands from God.*

Abram first traveled with his family from his home, Ur of the Chaldeans, to *Haran*, which means "road." This was the first of many

17

tests of faith Abram would encounter on his long journey. He had to say good-bye to his past if he chose to go father down the pathway of promise. I can imagine that, as he walked to the edge of the city each morning, Abram felt the pull of God's Promised Land—a place flowing with milk and honey. But returning to the home of an aged father, he hid the promises in his heart to live out the hours of another day.

Abram must have thought, *Do I see a new horizon? Or is it a spotlight keeping me in touch with reality? Where do I go from here?*

Haran was a crossroad of choices, a tug-of-war between:

- Disobedience and obedience
- Family and God
- Flesh and spirit
- Dreams and realities
- Old habits and new hope

With each day, Abram reminded himself that Canaan was waiting. The beckoning call of God tugged at his heart. Would this be the day to take the giant step of faith? Could he walk into his dying father's room and tell him he was leaving?

Days turned into months, months into years. Before Abram knew it, he had lived in Haran, the city of limbo, for five years—five years filled with dreaming and soul-searching. It wasn't until after the death and burial of his father, Terah, that Abram finally continued his pursuit of the promise.

THE LAND OF PROMISE

After traveling approximately 240 miles from Haran, Abram and his family came to Shechem, a city in Canaan. (See Genesis 12:4–6.) The small caravan approached the city with elation. The next morning Abram was led by the Spirit to a high place where God affirmed the promise: *"To your descendants I will give this land"* (verse 7). God was refining Abram's character in a pagan land infested with idolatry and wickedness. The people of Shechem were unaware of God's promise.

The great pastor Henry Ward Beecher said, "If a man cannot be a Christian in the place where he is, he cannot be a Christian anywhere." One might also say, "If a man cannot be *faithful* where he is, he will not be *faithful* anywhere." Abram clung to the vision God had given him. In the midst of ridicule, rejection, and isolation, Abram built altars and worshipped God. His dream of fulfilling God's promises burned brightly in his heart—until famine hit. With starving herds and a lack of food, Abram's faith was stretched to the limit. Would he hold on?

> *"If a man cannot be a Christian in the place where he is, he cannot be a Christian anywhere."*
> —Henry Ward Beecher

DOWN TO EGYPT—THE HIGH PRICE OF DISOBEDIENCE

Rumors from traveling caravans said there was plenty to eat in Egypt. Instead of trusting God, Abram began thinking about turning away from Canaan, taking the easy road by going *"down to Egypt"* (Genesis 12:10). Finally Abram announced to his family that they were indeed heading south.

Egypt represents the world's detour from God's promises. Abram's promise would never materialize in Egypt. His dreams and goals would die a slow death on the road of disobedience.

19

Abram's journey to Egypt was provoked by famine; however, he got into trouble with Pharaoh and was asked to leave the country. Later, Isaac was warned by God to stay out of Egypt. (See Genesis 26:2.) Many years later, Jacob and his sons would travel down to Egypt—once again, to avoid famine—at the invitation of Joseph, who had been elevated to rulership. (See Genesis 45:4–11.) After the famine and Joseph's death, however, the Israelites became slaves of Pharaoh. After 430 years of staying in Egypt, they were ready to leave.

The phrase *"down to Egypt"* is used sixteen times in the Bible, whereas Scripture refers to people going *"up out of Egypt"* thirty-three times. Disobedience always leads downward and away from God. God's plan for you and me is to live on higher ground—the rarefied air where eagles soar and nest on mountain peaks. God's plan also includes waiting and patience. *"But those who wait on the LORD shall renew their strength; they shall mount up with wings like eagles, they shall run and not be weary, they shall walk and not faint"* (Isaiah 40:31).

> *Disobedience is always a detour—a detour that withholds the promises of God in our lives.*

Disobedience is always a detour—a detour that withholds the promises of God in our lives. As a child, I was greatly influenced by a minister with a unique preaching and singing style. After many years, I lost touch with him. A few years ago, I heard the terrible news that this man was sent to prison for murder. After learning the details preceding this event, I realized that Egypt's call eventually enticed him. He left the ministry, his wife, and his ministerial calling to pursue the "things of this world" in Egypt. Recently, a pastor friend of mine visited him in prison. The ex-minister said to my friend, "Tell everyone you know, 'It's not worth it!' Tell them, 'Sin will take you farther than you ever thought you could go.'"

The chase cost him dearly. His total losses are unknown, but one thing is sure: he lost the season of blessings and promises preserved for this time in his life. As the old saying goes, "Sin will always take you farther than you want to go. Sin will always keep you longer than you want to stay. Sin will always cost you more than you can afford to pay."

Lord help me, my Children, Grand Children, great-grand Children

GOING DOWN TO EGYPT

PERSONAL EVALUATION

Read each of the following statements and answer **True** or **False**. After answering, take time to reflect on your answers to determine areas in your life that need prayer.

1. I truly believe that God has placed seeds of greatness in my life. True

2. I am pursuing God's promises in my life.

3. I understand areas of weakness (temptations) that could potentially lure me into this world's system, and I am guarding myself against them. True

4. I truly believe God has a plan for my life. True

5. I truly believe God wants me to win and not to lose. True

PERSONAL REFLECTION

Meditate on the following questions and answer them honestly.

1. Do I fully understand the high cost associated with disobeying God's plan for my life? True

2. Am I waiting for something to happen before I follow God's plan for my life? True

3. Am I fully aware that my disobedience may visit the generation that follows me unless I follow God's plan? True

4. Do I really believe God wants me to live in victory? True

5. Have I claimed the promises of God for my life? Not yet.

GROUP DISCUSSION

1. Abraham is one of the greatest Old Testament patriarchs and Bible heroes. Discuss Abram, the ordinary man, and his struggles to take God at His word.

2. Name several promises of God and discuss how they apply to your current situation.

3. Ask a member of the group to share a personal experience of being at a crossroads.

4. Some people believe that the spiritual analogy of the Promised Land or Canaan is heaven. Explain.

5. Discuss why you think it is God's will for each person to be an overcomer.

6. List and discuss some of the seeds of greatness God has placed within each of us.

7. Discuss the last three sentences in this chapter:

   • Sin will always take you farther than you want to go.

   • Sin will always keep you longer than you want to stay.

   • Sin will always cost you more than you can afford to pay.

GROUP EXERCISE

Arrange your chairs in a circle. Take turns as members of the group point out some seeds of greatness God has placed in each individual's life. The result will be positive and powerful as you see exhortation and encouragement personified.

chapter 2

Passing Under in order to Pass Over

(handwritten: 8.7.2011 my day out of Egypt, out of the house of Bondage!)

The Story of the Passover

And it came to pass, on that very same day, that the LORD brought the children of Israel out of the land of Egypt according to their armies. Then the LORD spoke to Moses, saying, "Consecrate to Me all the firstborn, whatever opens the womb among the children of Israel, both of man and beast; it is Mine." And Moses said to the people: "Remember this day in which you went out of Egypt, out of the house of bondage; for by strength of hand the LORD brought you out of this place. No leavened bread shall be eaten. "On this day you are going out, in the month Abib. "And it shall be, when the LORD brings you into the land of the Canaanites and the Hittites and the Amorites and the Hivites and the Jebusites, which He swore to your fathers to give you, a land flowing with milk and honey, that you shall keep this service in this month." (Exodus 12:51–13:5)

The Israelites went "down to Egypt" to escape famine, never intending to stay the length of time they actually did. They became comfortable in their new surroundings.

(handwritten: I Became comfortable In my surroundings Still Calls me back!)

Their families grew and prospered under Joseph's rulership. This comfort quickly ended, however, when both Joseph and the pharaoh died. The people of Israel—these descendants of Abraham, as Abram was now called—became slaves of the new pharaoh. They began to long and pray for their freedom and deliverance. They had grown familiar and comfortable in Egypt; now, however, they were slaves, and God had to awaken them in order to get them out of Egypt. *I also bengan to long and Pray for my fruedom,*

FROM FAMINE TO FAMILIARITY

Familiarity will disable our destiny and shroud our promise in fog, leaving us confused, frustrated, and disconnected. Worse than famine, it lulls us to sleep in several ways: *going and comin*

1) Familiarity is the thief of dreams. As each day takes on the flavor of yesterday, the spinning wheel of life turns so steadily you forget to get off. Like a soaring buzzard with no place to land, the "sameness" of the world becomes like a drive across Kansas in the summer. Each field and farm looks just like the ones you passed during the last hundred miles. Soon you stop looking. Soon the vision is gone. Hope and optimism leave with it, but we're not quite sure when. *lost my Vision,*

Vision not only guides our future, but it also helps us see the present more clearly. Without vision we walk through life as a blind man with no guide—taking the same turns, making the same mistakes, recreating the same old scenarios. Soon we can't even remember what life was like before.

2) Familiarity robs us of freshness that makes each day new and turns each laugh into a treasure.

3. Familiarity drowns out the music of life, washing away the encouraging, melodious words of family, friends, and God. In time,

even those closest to us seem like strangers. And the most distant person in our world is the man in the mirror. *looked for me in the mirror*

4. Familiarity blinds us to the dangers of complacency, placidity, and routine. Life now seems to be painted with a coat of beige where all things blend. The things that were once considered threats to our future are common and perhaps even comrades in this new world of the familiar.

SATAN HAD A PLOT, BUT GOD HAD A PLAN

Israel, once a proud and blessed people, became oppressed with the daily struggles of slavery. The horrifying sights and sounds of whips cracking, people shouting, and children carrying twigs for the fire—all these comprised the long days and short nights of slavery. Separation from family members taxed the human spirit. As a nation they cried out to their God for a redeemer who would save them from this torturous life. How and when would God hear their cries?

Vision not only guides our future, but it also helps us see the present more clearly.

The arrival of their redeemer was a shock to all. How could Moses, the adopted son of the princess, the one who killed an Egyptian guard, a fugitive with a price on his head, be their deliverer? Fortunately, God doesn't consult the past to determine the future for those whom He calls. God used a series of plagues to strike fear into the hearts of the Egyptians and to establish Moses as His deliverer in the eyes of the Israelites.

Even today, God has an exit door for every person who ends up in Egypt. Whether He chooses to use a fugitive like Moses, a lionhearted shepherd like David, or a rough outdoorsman like John the Baptist, God has a plan! He often uses the ordinary to do the extraordinary. His plan today may not include ten plagues and an "angel of death," but He has a way of delivering anyone willing to leave the land of mediocrity and despair. *I am willing*

Can God Get Me Out?

Headlines declared, "Plane Shot Down—Pilot Lost." Dread swept the nation in 1995 as we learned of twenty-nine-year-old air force Captain Scott O'Grady, who ejected when his fighter jet was shot down in the "no-fly zone" over Serbian-held Bosnia. Surviving on insects and wild plants, he cautiously waited for the well-trained rescue team who eventually blasted in and out in two minutes to take him home.

Many others who are rescued daily from a life of imprisonment never make headlines. Missionary Dean Galyen, recounting his journeys through Africa, tells the story of a lady in Rwanda who was forced to kill her neighbor and her neighbor's three children. This woman asked, "Can your God really save someone like me?" The answer is, unequivocally, "Yes!"

War has a way of corrupting and twisting the minds of the innocent. On one of my annual trips into the Central American country of El Salvador, I encountered a young man whom I will call Carlos. He, too, survived on insects and plants, fighting for the national army in their heinous civil war. He related stories of how he chopped off men's heads and sewed them up inside their bellies as a political demonstration. Tearfully, he poured out his soul relating how he murdered men while they were pleading and begging for their lives. With weary eyes, he disclosed volumes of untold stories, exposing windows into the chained and tormented state of his soul. He also asked the question, "Can your God really save a man like me?"

Again, the answer was, and still is, "Yes!" With the help of a Spanish interpreter, Carlos knelt in a room filled with American construction workers and asked Jesus Christ into his life. Today he lives his life for God.

John was a drug user and a thief. He dropped out of school, had two children out of wedlock, and was in and out of every juvenile court in the city. He had no religious background. His language was profane; his appearance was back-alley street attire. Society had given up on John and stereotyped him as a psychotic sociopath. When I met him, only one person believed in

> *God has a way of delivering anyone willing to leave the land of mediocrity and despair.*

him. That one person came out of her own Egypt but went back for John. She is a real heroine. She walked the aisle with John twice, once to meet Jesus, and the other in matrimony. Today John is a healthy, productive Christian. He is a father, a hard worker, and a loving husband—free from the fears of tomorrow. He, too, got out of Egypt.

ORDINARY PEOPLE, ORDINARY THINGS

Look at these attributes: simple, stuttering, scared, scorched, selfless, and sore. Do these describe a hero to you? Moses was all these things, and yet he was the deliverer of the Israelites.

One of the greatest soulwinners I know is just a simple man. I have never seen him in a suit. His speech is common. He began his own ministry, the Stranded Motorist Ministry. While going to and from his work as a prison guard, he stops to help motorists who are stranded. As he works on their cars, he proclaims the good news of the Gospel and gives them a sermon on cassette tape. Through his ministry, people have been healed, saved, and delivered because someone pointed the way "out of Egypt." It's a simple message and method, proclaimed by a simple man.

Although Moses was used mightily by God, all he really did was hold up the exit sign. God has a road sign for every weary traveler. The message is always the same: "Turn right and keep going straight." Egypt gets confusing and complicated with its many roads and multiple choices. It's easy to get lost in Egypt, but the way out is still simple.

THROUGH THE BLOOD AND READY TO GO

Moses declared to the Israelites, in effect, "The only way out of Egypt is through the blood." (See Exodus 12:1–23.) Each household had to sacrifice an unblemished male lamb in its first year, then take a hyssop branch and smear its blood upon the doorpost. Next, they were to sit down and eat the lamb's meat with unleavened bread and bitter herbs. While eating, the family had to be ready to leave at any time. After packing and arraying their doorpost with blood, the Israelites ate the Passover lamb, gathered the family together, and remained in their clothes and shoes. (See verse 11.) They did not know when their Deliverer would call, so they had to be ready.

> *It's easy to get lost in Egypt, but the way out is still simple: "Turn right and keep going straight."*

Imagine the scene. The moon hung low in a reddish wake. The king's palace was silent with the exception of chatter among the guards. Then God unzipped the veil separating the temporary from the eternal, enough for the "angel of death" to step through. Silence hovered over the land as sleeping babes and grown men—the firstborn of each household—died in their sleep. As daylight broke, cries and screams could be heard from house to house. Women ran into the streets with dead babies, cursing the God of the Israelites. They also cursed Pharaoh, their king, for resisting God and allowing this plague to come upon them.

That same morning, Moses and Aaron were awakened—not by an angel, but rather by an angry guard who dragged them to the Pharaoh's chambers. Holding his dead son in his arms, the angry king ordered the Israelites to leave. The curses of the distraught queen mother could be heard as they hurried to the slave city of Goshen.

When the Israelites heard the prearranged signal, they launched into action, harnessed their oxen, and lined their carts in a row. At last it was time to get out of Egypt. (See Exodus 12:29–33.)

As the Israelites began to walk out of Egypt, they felt what every sinner feels walking toward the altar. They walked past the head slave master who was powerless to stop them. The Egyptians willingly gave the jewelry from their bodies to the Hebrew slaves as they marched out. Imagine a slave taking the signet ring (a signature of power) right off the hand of the head slave master. You can almost imagine Moses turning as they left and saying, "Stop! Take one last look at Egypt and never forget what a life of slavery is like."

Next came the real test: now that they were out of Egypt, would they ever be able to get Egypt out of them? Part of experiencing freedom is the joy and thankfulness that come from remembering what God delivered you out of and where you were when He found you. *I was sad- unhappy, fearful.*

GETTING OUT OF EGYPT

my sin took me there. Replied me there too

The plight of sin is bondage, and it is not something we can escape by ourselves. It requires a Deliverer. God has raised up many servants to point the way, but the ultimate Deliverer is Jesus.

Yes. Jesus.

31

Egypt is always waiting with its enticements and charms. But so is the promise of Canaan. Egypt and Canaan coexist in our world today. Egypt, a secular society with its system of selfishness, still enslaves many with the chains of hopelessness and despair. Their lives are beaten down by the taskmasters of societal expectations and peer pressure. The taskmaster exists in many forms:

- The taskmaster of workaholism robs us of time needed for personal growth and relationship development.
- The taskmaster of fear robs us of opportunities and personal achievement.
- The taskmaster of low self-esteem robs us of our self-worth.
- The taskmaster of memories of our past failures rob us of our future success.
- The taskmaster of anger robs us of joy.
- The taskmaster of jealousy robs us of security.

Many remain enslaved. The historical figure of Pharaoh is no longer on the throne, but the spirit of antichrist rules in his stead, dictating degrading morals and unethical codes of conduct. The king is still wicked and the people are still in bondage.

In the midst of this confusion and gloom, a light shines through with the promise that will lead you to Canaan:

- The land of inheritance and ownership
- The land of victory and fruitfulness
- The land where the Deliverer, Jesus Christ, is King
- A place where giants fall and walls crumble

Canaan is not free of challenge or peril, yet it stands as a symbol of victory where you can win over trouble and despair. In Canaan, you find a land for overcomers, a land of rejoicing and praise. In Canaan, God goes before you into battle. He is your banner, your rock, your fortress, your buckler, and your high tower—a place the righteous run to for safety. (See 1 Chronicles 14:15, Psalm 91:2–4, Proverbs 18:10, Exodus 17:15, 2 Samuel 22:2–3.)

You do not have to be a slave to sin any longer. Get up and get out of Egypt. The plan is still the same: there is a doorway covered with the blood of an unblemished Lamb. Walk through that door and follow Him to the Land of Promise. God designed you to be a winner. You weren't created for Egypt; you were created for Canaan. You weren't created to be a slave; you were created to be a conqueror.

Come on, let's go to Canaan.

Out of Egypt unto my Canaan...Promies land..

GETTING SIN OUT OF ME

PERSONAL EVALUATION

Read each of the following statements and answer **True** or **False**. Then consider the questions that follow.

1. I have become complacent about some of the important people in my life, thus not appreciating them for their value to me. Who are some people you should appreciate more? Childre···

2. There are things in my life I have tolerated that I know I should change. What is the first thing you would change? Get so ob a bad Marriage

3. I know that I am saved because I have believed in Jesus Christ as my Savior and Lord.

4. I haven't forgotten from where God has delivered me. What are some of the things that God has delivered you from? my Sulb.

5. I am comfortable around things I know are sinful. What are some temptations that you should be more cautious of?

PERSONAL REFLECTION

Meditate on the following questions and answer honestly.

1. Do I fully realize not only what God saved me from, but also what He saved me from becoming?

    Yes!

2. Does sin make me uncomfortable, or is it so familiar to me that I am complacent about it?

3. Do I consider myself a Christian, or am I in the
   process of becoming a Christian?

GROUP DISCUSSION

1. The Israelites went "down to Egypt," never intending to stay. How does this compare to ways in
   which we may be in danger of dabbling in sin?

2. Discuss the following symbols mentioned in the
   Exodus story and what they represent in New
   Testament salvation:

   Moses the deliverer vs. Pharaoh

   an unblemished lamb

   the blood of the lamb

   blood on the doorposts

   unleavened bread

   bitter herbs

   the passing over of the Lord

   the exodus from Egypt

3. Discuss the benefit of remembering where God
   has brought you from.   *Bondage to Condepen/cers*

4. Discuss the danger of forgetting where God has
   brought you from.

5. Moses was a simple and humble man whom
   God used to be the Old Testament *type of Christ.*

Name modern-day ordinary men who could be classified as heroes of the faith.

6. Have someone in the group tell the story of his or her salvation experience.

Group Exercise

Do a role-playing exercise to explain the plan of salvation to someone who has never heard the gospel message.

We must first change our minds to do when we have to do war against the enemy to so bad and want to Egypt.

chapter 3

GOING THROUGH THE VALLEY TO GET DELIVERANCE

CAMPING AT THE VALLEY OF SUCCOTH AND ETHAM

Then it came to pass, when Pharaoh had let the people go, that God did not lead them by way of the land of the Philistines, although that was near; for God said, "Lest perhaps the people change their minds when they see war, and return to Egypt." So God led the people around by way of the wilderness of the Red Sea. And the children of Israel went up in orderly ranks out of the land of Egypt. (Exodus 13:17–18)

D o the following statements sound like empty phrases or incredible faith?

- *"Here am I! Send me."* (Isaiah 6:8)
- "Where He leads me, I will follow." (E. W. Blandly)
- "I am Thine, O Lord, I have heard Thy voice." (Fanny J. Crosby)

- "I have decided to follow Jesus, no turning back, no turning back." (traditional hymn)

The intent of each of God's children is to follow Him unconditionally, even when adversity comes. That is when we learn the difference between God's point of view and man's. God sees the overall picture from beginning to end. We try to see; we strain our reasoning trying to understand, but at best we can see only the present, which is merely a glimpse of the big picture. "Follow Me" was the initial instruction Jesus gave His disciples in the early ministry years. "Follow Me" was the implied instruction given to Abraham, Moses, and Joshua. Sometimes the only instruction we get from the Lord is "Follow Me."

> **God is trying to mold our character. He is more interested in the finished product than in the comfort of a single day.**

Jesus said, *"Follow Me, and I will make you fishers of men"* (Matthew 4:19). No further details, just "Follow Me." Jesus wanted to make disciples of all who would follow Him. God said to Moses, in essence, "Follow Me, and I will turn the heart of Pharaoh. I will draw him to a place I have prepared for him and his army." Faith becomes all the more difficult when we leave God and His promises out of the equation.

IS THIS THE RIGHT WAY, GOD?

Canaan was only an eighteen-day journey from Egypt. Merchants and other travelers to and from Egypt had made the journey before. It may have been a desert, but it was not uncharted territory. Yet, God did not lead the Israelites on the direct route. Instead, He told Moses to lead this fearful caravan into the wilderness. They could have remained in Egypt, but they followed their Deliverer and went with the faith that says, "God feeds where He leads."

God knows where you are headed, and He knows where He must take you to get you there. God's leadership is long-term. He is not interested in our shortcut systems. God is trying to mold our character. He is more interested in the finished product than in the comfort of a single day. That is why the apostle Paul later said, *"All things work together for good to those who love God, to those who are the called according to His purpose"* (Romans 8:28). This is not to suggest that all the things that work together are necessarily "good" or "pleasant" things. Like a giant jigsaw puzzle, the portrait of who we are is formed in His divine plan for our lives. Each circumstance we encounter may not seem to have a significant purpose, but when God writes the final chapter, He will pull it all together in two words: "Well done!" (See, for example, Matthew 25:21.)

HIS WAYS ARE ABOVE OUR WAYS

Many years ago, while sitting in a missions service, I was challenged to go to the country of El Salvador, which was in the midst of a brutal civil war, making it difficult for missionaries to enter. Nevertheless, I made my plans to go and found six brave souls to accompany me. The urge to go was simply more overwhelming to me than the uncertainty.

Two weeks before our departure, I received word that the guerrilla forces had sent a threatening notice to the man who would serve as our contact. They were demanding $20,000 (U.S. currency) in exchange for letting our contact live. After being notified, the members of my team all felt the situation was too risky, so they backed out. I, too, was tempted to remain at home, but the call kept ringing in my ears to go. Many advised me to cancel my plans, but I knew in my heart that I was supposed to go.

The day came for me to fly to El Salvador alone. I really didn't know what to expect. Upon arriving, I was abruptly greeted by a brusque group of soldiers. They frisked me, disassembled my camera, and poked me with their guns while others rifled through my luggage. There were many days during my stay when I questioned the Lord about my presence there. Each evening I was locked behind six iron doors in a room with no ventilation. We had to disinfect and debug the room each evening, which meant going to sleep breathing insecticide. I would lie awake sweating, listening to gunfire, screams, and planes flying overhead. I visited churches that had been bombed and spoke with pastors whose family members had been killed.

> *God was calling me to open the door so hundreds of short-term missionaries could go into the country and build up His kingdom.*

When the trip was finally over, I was exhausted, dehydrated, and briefly hospitalized. I was glad I had gone, but I really had no definite plans to return. Approximately one year later, I heard the same voice drawing me again. I fought the feeling for many months. Finally, I said yes to God and began to make plans for a second trip to the country.

By this time, the country's government had signed a peace treaty with the rebel forces. Once again I made an appeal for short-term missionaries. This time, to my amazement, thirty-two people signed up to go. While there, we built a church building in only eight days. We were the first American team from our denomination to build a church in El Salvador. Since then, we have gone back every year to build another church.

God wasn't calling me to make a fearful, one-time visit. He was calling me to open the door so hundreds of short-term missionaries could go into the country and build up His kingdom.

DETOURS

Then it came to pass, when Pharaoh had let the people go, that God did not lead them by way of the land of the Philistines, although that was near; for God said, "Lest perhaps the people change their minds when they see war, and return to Egypt."

(Exodus 13:17)

Premature blessings. Do such things exist? In our world of "instant everything," we sometimes forget that quality takes time. The people of Israel simply were not ready to handle the challenges of Canaan. That was the purpose for this "boot camp" in the desert. They weren't being punished—they were being trained.

Can you imagine how life would turn out if God answered every prayer the way we asked Him to? God would not be in control anymore—we would. He would be our "genie in a bottle," catering to our every whim and desire. There would be no dependence, no trust, no faith, no growth, no personal development, no transformation, no molding or reshaping, and no character. God would be in the hands of man, instead of man being in the hands of God.

God told the Israelites,

I will not drive them out from before you in one year, lest the land become desolate and the beast of the field become too numerous for you. Little by little I will drive them out from before you, until you have increased, and you inherit the land.

(Exodus 23:29–30)

Little by little—that is how success is achieved. Not one big win, but many small wins compounded. Dr. Mike Murdock says, "The secret to success is found in our daily routine." God knows this and is trying to teach us to win, little by little.

If God delays us, it is only to get our eyes off ourselves and back on Him and His promise. Satan, however, strives to detour us from reaching our goals. He sidetracks us with selfish interests so that we lose our way.

Detours—things that deter your focus and defer your interest—may change your entire course or direction. Delays are only learning experiences to help you focus more aptly on the journey. The difference between a detour and a delay is simple: when the direction in which you are moving takes you away from your desired goal, it's a *detour*; when it complements and corresponds with your destination, then it is simply a *delay*.

HE LEADS ME TO AND THROUGH THE VALLEY

There are plenty of mountains in God's kingdom, just as there are plenty of grassy meadows, rippling brooks, and fertile valleys. Why valleys? God led the Israelites to camp at the Valley of Succoth, just before the Red Sea. Psalm 23 gives us fresh insight about valleys:

The LORD is my shepherd; I shall not want. He makes me to lie down in green pastures; He leads me beside the still waters. He restores my soul; He leads me in the paths of righteousness for His name's sake. Yea, though I walk through the valley of the shadow of death, I will fear no evil; for You are with me; Your rod and Your staff, they comfort me. You prepare a table before me in the presence of my enemies; You anoint my head with oil; my cup runs over. Surely goodness and mercy shall follow me all the days of my life; and I will dwell in the house of the LORD forever.

(Psalm 23:1–6)

Notice that *"He leads me beside the still waters."* This is the way of peace. Here, *"He restores my soul."* Also, *"He leads me in the paths of righteousness"*—not highways, not sidewalks, not even trails, but paths. Worn-down places where few have trod. Places that few have seen, with fruit that few have tasted, and scenery that few have seen.

Then, He leads me *"through the valley."* If He leads you *to* the valley, He'll take you *through* the valley. In the valley, I find:

- A place to remember.
- A place to stop.
- A place to be still and know God.
- A place to meet Him.

The Valley of Succoth had a distinct purpose. In the valley, God's people heard Him speak. The valley is the place where we are restored and refreshed for the journey ahead.

In the valley, we remember what God has brought us from: sin, bondage, slavery. When we remember what God delivered us from, we will declare not only what He saved us from, but also what He saved us from becoming. We may not be what we want to be, but thank God we're not *what we could have been.*

NEXT STOP: ETHAM

So they took their journey from Succoth and camped in Etham at the edge of the wilderness. And the LORD went before them by day in a pillar of cloud to lead the way, and by night in a pillar of fire to give them light, so as to go by day and night. He did not take away the pillar of cloud by day or the pillar of fire by night from before the people. (Exodus 13:20–22)

Etham is where God made Himself visible to the nation of Israel. The scene was both a frightening and glorious sight. First, the wind increased in velocity like a race car revving its engines. The sun darkened as the air became thin. Clouds rolled in huge billows as if they were boiling from a furnace. The ground shook, not like an earthquake, but with a steady quiver.

Suddenly, a *Shekinah* cloud—the visible manifestation of God's glorious presence on earth—began to spiral from the heavens to the place where the Hebrews were camped. As it touched the ground, it grew and took on the shape of a huge column. Once formed, it stood majestically, a pillar made of clouds. This Shekinah was so bright that it was hard to look upon. It glowed as though a fire were burning within it. The people knew God was in their midst.

This indescribable image of God's presence was displayed in two significant forms—a *pillar of cloud* and a *pillar of fire*. The Hebrew word for *pillar* is *ammuwd*, which means "a standing column." The purpose of a pillar is to hold something up. Suddenly, in the desert, they discovered that the burden of this journey was not all up to them.

FAITH HOLDS UP THE MAN
WHO HOLDS UP THE FAITH

There is a song that says, in essence, that we do not know our future, but we do know who holds our future. What stupendous truth lies in this profound phrase.

David and Mary Haynes had their faith put to the test. They raised a beautiful family and instilled in them the truths of God. Their middle daughter, Leatha, married a pastor, Rick Whitter. The

Haynes family was then blessed with two beautiful granddaughters. When their youngest granddaughter was only three years old, she was diagnosed with a rare type of cancer called *neuroblastoma*.

David and Mary decided to stay with Rick and Leatha in order to enter into a time of spiritual warfare. Daily, David walked the floor of a twelve-by-fourteen-foot room, praying hour upon hour. Each evening, however, he noticed the girl's condition continue to worsen. He intensified the prayer time and coupled it with fasting. All four adults entered into intense personal "war-prayer." Convinced that God would not let them down, they prayed fervently to the point of exhaustion.

This battle continued for ninety days. As they sat in their Florida home just two days after her fourth birthday, they watched the life slowly leave this little girl. David Haynes picked up his Bible and for a moment was tempted to throw it out, but instead he clung to it. The months passed, the pain diminished somewhat, but the questions and doubt lingered. Satan thought he had finally detoured David and Mary Haynes.

> *David Haynes picked up his Bible and for a moment was tempted to throw it out, but instead he clung to it.*

At a church service a few months later, I asked David to pray for those who had come forward. As I handed the microphone to him, I saw his countenance change. All at once the most powerful prayer I have ever heard burst from his lips. The more he prayed, the more powerful it became. Each person who came up for prayer that morning was delivered. I watched as a mighty prayer warrior was birthed through an adverse situation.

45

Since then, David has been on missionary trips where God has performed miracles through his prayers. One day, while on a work site in a foreign country, he prayed in agreement with another brother and saw three distinct miracles in one afternoon.

In 1994, while in El Salvador, David Haynes prayed for God's intervention because the only water source we had was being rationed. On one clear evening, clouds suddenly formed, and it rained enough to fill every water barrel and basin. National Overseer David Peraza, a native El Salvadorian, told us it was the first time in his life he had ever seen it rain in late February—a full three months after the rainy season is over.

Faith holds up the man who holds up the faith!

GETTING OUT OF THE VALLEY

PERSONAL EVALUATION

Read each of the following statements and answer **True** or **False**.

1. I truly believe I am following God as He leads me on a spiritual journey.
2. I have complete faith that God is in control of my life.
3. I can accept a "no" answer from God.
4. I can sense God's presence In the valleys of my life.
5. I am determined to keep the faith, no matter what.

PERSONAL REFLECTION

Meditate on the following questions and answer them honestly.

1. Do I truly know how to follow God as He leads the way?
2. Can I accept the fact that a premature blessing could do more harm to me than good and that I should trust God to bless me as I mature in Him?

3. Do I view each valley as a learning experience or as a delay in my spiritual walk?

4. Even though I may never see a pillar of fire or a *Shekinah* cloud, do I see God in other ways? How?

5. Do I trust God even when it is inconvenient?

GROUP DISCUSSION

1. Discuss how we can know the difference between God's leading and following after our own plans.

2. Discuss the danger of a premature blessing.

3. Have a member of the group share a personal experience of a lesson learned in the valley.

4. Read and discuss Exodus 23:29–30.

5. The *"pillar of cloud"* and *"pillar of fire"* imagery of God is important because it signifies that God is the column that is holding up the spiritual building. How can we relate to that image in our day? Is God still a pillar of fire in the desert?

6. Discuss the difference between a test of faith and a temptation.

7. Discuss what our Christian character would be like if we never had a valley or a testing of our faith. How long would it take before we became spoiled children who pitched tantrums to get God's attention?

GROUP EXERCISE

Have each member of the group write a letter to a discouraged friend who is presently in the valley. If the friend responds positively, ask his or her permission to read the response to the group. Everyone will be able to share in the ministry of encouragement, as well as the victory of overcoming.

PART II

THE WILDERNESS
AND HOW
TO GET THROUGH

THE WILDERNESS

Getting up is the hardest part. Overcoming inertia and apathy and defeat is the beginning of deliverance. Ask anyone who has been through addiction recovery. Ask anyone who has started an exercise regimen. Ask anyone who has followed his or her dreams and started a business. Getting started is the hardest part—but it's not the only part.

Often, after you begin comes the desert. The desert is many things to many people. It is the place of hard work and character refinement. It is the place of self-discovery and healing. It is the place of training and developing new skills. It is the place where you will be tested and tempted to give up. But most of all, it is the place where you discard the old ways of thinking that got you nowhere.

But if you make it through, you will be transformed and strengthened to fulfill your calling and vision. How long it takes will be, in part, up to you. With faith and obedience, it could be a quick trip. If rebellion and bad attitudes set in, it could take years. That is why it is so crucial that we learn the lessons of getting through the wilderness.

chapter 4

GETTING RID OF THE PAST

CAMPING AT MIGDOL AND THE RED SEA

So he [Pharaoh] made ready his chariot and took his people with him. Also, he took six hundred choice chariots, and all the chariots of Egypt with captains over every one of them. And the LORD hardened the heart of Pharaoh king of Egypt, and he pursued the children of Israel; and the children of Israel went out with boldness. So the Egyptians pursued them, all the horses and chariots of Pharaoh, his horsemen and his army, and overtook them camping by the sea beside Pi Hahiroth, before Baal Zephon. And when Pharaoh drew near, the children of Israel lifted their eyes, and behold, the Egyptians marched after them. So they were very afraid, and the children of Israel cried out to the LORD. (Exodus 14:6–10)

You open the door. The light is dim. Everything is covered in last year's dust, including out-of-style clothing that now looks silly. The handmade sentimentalities are barely recognizable. There is your diary and an old toy, but you still haven't found what you're looking for.

Digging through the old newspapers and worn-out shoes, you finally see it underneath an empty candy box you thought might come in handy one day. At last, the old shoe box filled with photos is recovered. These photos captured all those silly hairdos, toothless children, embittered frowns, and playful smiles. This is the past.

Some photos bring back joyful memories. Other memories, you just wish someone would throw away. One photo makes you laugh. Another brings a tear. Suddenly, you find one you forgot was there and the pain starts all over again. How can a photo bring on such a flood of emotions? There you are with a faded photo in your hand, and a hidden file of memories bursts open in your mind. It's the past, with all its mistakes, failures, trouble, pain, hurts, and disappointments—an old mental file sealed years ago. It has resurfaced. Wouldn't it be nice to hold on to all the good memories while burying the painful, destructive ones once and for all?

ISRAEL'S PAST

Can you imagine what hundreds of years of slavery do to a culture? Generations had endured the hardships of the whipping post, a slave's portion of food, and a straw bed. Women were valued only for their ability to bear more children—more slave labor. It was "captivity thinking." No wonder God wasn't ready to give them Canaan. Not yet. He could deliver them from the slave master's whip, but they still had the mentality of slaves, not conquerors.

Was Caleb ready to say, *"Give me this mountain,"* as he would later in Joshua 14:12? Could a teenaged Joshua say, *"As for me and my house, we will serve the LORD"* (Joshua 24:15)? Their fathers, grandfathers, and great-grandfathers were slaves before them. This was the only way of life they knew. Their potential lay dormant, exposed to only one way of thinking—a thinking they had to get rid of.

Getting out was the first step to discovering the champion inside. But what about the slave masters? Would God's people always be looking over their shoulders to see if these abusers were creeping up on them again?

LIVING LIFE IN THE REARVIEW MIRROR

Too many of God's children live defeated lives because they allow the past and their fears to hover over their heads like dark clouds. Even when doors open to the future, these people remain chained to their pasts. They walk as through a minefield, never knowing which step will blow their cover and expose the past. This heinous monster visits them in their sleep. On the outside, they are smiling, but on the inside, scenes from the past are on continuous play. If only someone could turn off the past and make it go away.

Too many of God's children live defeated lives because they allow the past and their fears to hover over their heads like dark clouds.

A young lady whom I will call Jackie came to my office crying, heaving up years of emotional pain and guilt. Most of her problems stemmed from severe abuse during adolescence. During our sessions I asked her to close her eyes, clear her thoughts, and detail a normal day in her life at the age of ten. This sensitive exercise broke her down as it exposed a heart still gripped by pain and fear.

In the same manner, I asked her to detail her activities on that present day. Things had changed. Her day began at 6 a.m. with children to feed, a husband's lunch to make, clothes to wash, a house to clean, and an appointment with me to keep. I followed the exercise with a question: "What is the difference?"

"Things have changed," she said. "I have changed."

The magic of that moment was instrumental in freeing her from the grip of her painful past. She was a grown woman who didn't realize that her life was still dominated by memories of the past. We must be free from the past in order to live in the present.

THE DEVIL IN MY REARVIEW MIRROR

Satan wants to haunt us with our pasts through the mechanism of worry. He uses it as a weapon of intimidation, twisting the facts and causing us to fret about incidentals that are magnified out of proportion. He uses our God-given gift of imagination to create very unrealistic scenarios.

This is why the Word of God instructs us to use the weapons of our warfare against Satan in *"casting down imaginations, and every high thing that exalteth itself against the knowledge of God, and bringing into captivity every thought to the obedience of Christ"* (2 Corinthians 10:5 KJV).

Another way Satan uses our pasts against us is by reminding us of our failures in life. Failure is a part of life everyone experiences. When God forgives us of failure, we must forgive ourselves so that Satan cannot reload the ammunition to use against us.

Rahab was a prostitute in Jericho. Her family was the only one spared in Israel's conquest of the city. She married an Israelite and became an adopted ancestor of Jesus. You will find her name mentioned in Matthew's account of the genealogy of Christ. (See Matthew 1:5.)

Many of God's mighty men of valor had failures in their lives. According to Scripture,

- Abraham lied.
- Isaac lied.

- Jacob lied and deceived.
- Moses murdered.
- David murdered and committed adultery.
- Solomon allowed idolatry.
- Elijah doubted and feared man rather than God.
- Peter denied Christ.
- Paul killed Christians.

For some, their actions and failures had ramifications for their futures. David's homicidal and adulterous activities led to the death of his baby. Solomon's building of altars to the gods of his pagan wives led to disaster in a weak and divided Israel. God doesn't promise to protect us from the consequences of our actions. On the other hand, none of these men was disqualified for being used by God in the future because of the failures in his past.

THE CAMP OF MIGDOL AND THE RED SEA

Migdol represents a place of fear and helplessness. The sea is in front of you. The enemy is behind you. Mountains are on both sides. You are boxed in, trapped. Stress builds up. Hopelessness sets in. Anxieties mount. Anger builds. This is Migdol—the place where Israel confronted her past. God told Moses to have the people do three things (see Exodus 14:13–14):

1. Stand still.
2. See God.
3. Hold your peace.

Stand Still

Pharaoh's army was approaching. "Stand still." You could taste the dust from the fast-moving chariots. "Stand still." The sounds of hooves were beating in their ears. "Stand still." Voices cried out, "There is no place to run." "We're trapped!" "We're doomed!"

Moses answered back, "Stand still!"

Mothers clutched their children close. Fathers picked up a tool or a shepherd's staff as their only means of defense. The cattle were scurrying restlessly. The approaching horde shook the ground. Before them, the fifteen-mile stretch of sea was too long to swim. The mountains were too steep to climb. Families huddled together in shock and dread.

> *Doing nothing does not mean we go into denial or ignore our responsibilities.*

Sometimes, the only direction we get from the Lord is to stop and stand still. We view life with a new perspective when we stop. I once tried to videotape my wife's hometown from a moving vehicle. The footage came out blurred and meaningless. Similarly, our lives also get out of focus when we forget to stop. It is easy to think that the cure for every battle is to do something. Sometimes, however, the only orders we get from God are to do nothing.

Doing nothing does not mean we go into denial. It does not mean we ignore our responsibilities. Sometimes God wants us to stop long enough to regain our focus. In the chaos of confusion, stopping settles the dust and allows us time to revisit our original motives and intentions. Stopping helps us to see what God is doing.

See God

God is everywhere, but we have to look for Him. Those who seek God will find Him in every circumstance of life. You can't see God until you are still.

In 1995, I was diagnosed with enlarged nodules on my vocal cords and advised to have them surgically removed. The surgery would involve having my vocal cords stripped so that new skin could grow back. The worst part for me was that I would not be able to speak a word for three weeks while my vocal cords healed. All I would be able to do was whisper. For a minister who preaches five to seven times a week to be told he could not say a word for one whole month was bad news!

I went in for surgery and began my month of silence. During that month I discovered a whole new world I never knew existed. My seventy-hour work week had kept me too busy talking to stop and listen. I was too busy asking God to make *my* dreams come true to see *His* dreams for my life. Amazingly, I began to see things God's way. In the quietness I could meditate on His goodness and allow Him to open my spiritual eyes so that I could see with His vision.

Many years ago, American astronauts and Russian cosmonauts were asked if they experienced God while in space. The cosmonauts' conclusion was, "We looked everywhere and we did not see any sign of God." The astronauts' conclusion was different: "Everywhere we looked we saw God. The universe was filled with signs of His presence."

Hold Your Peace

Imagine that! The enemy was charging and God told the Israelites to hold their peace. Isn't peace the feeling we get at the end of the day when we prop up our feet and refresh ourselves with a cold drink? Or perhaps it is the feeling of getting the children in bed and then, finally, soaking in a hot bath.

Actually, that's not *peace;* that is only *relaxation.* God wasn't asking the Israelites to kick back and take it easy. He wasn't asking them to ignore the approaching army. He was asking them not to give up in defeat.

Two artists were once asked to paint a picture depicting peace. One great artist painted an eight-year-old boy sitting in a fishing boat on a perfectly calm lake. It symbolized peace as the absence of problems.

The other artist painted a gigantic waterfall whose ferocious and threatening waters avalanched off the side of a steep cliff. Hanging over the cliff was the branch of a tree with a bird's nest filled with eggs. The spray of the water rose just a few feet from the nest. This symbolized peace as a reliance on something greater than ourselves (in this case, the tree) in the midst of the threat.

I agree with the second artist.

- Peace is not found on a calm lake; it is seeing the Master walking on the water in the midst of a choppy sea. (See Mark 6:48–51.)

- Peace is not staying home and tending sheep; it is walking onto the battlefield with a slingshot in one hand, a stone in the other, and God in your sights. (See 1 Samuel 17:48–49.)

- Peace is not sitting at the king's right hand; it is walking in the furnace with the fourth man. (See Daniel 3:20–25.)

Peace does not come free of peril. *"You will keep him in perfect peace, whose mind is stayed on You"* (Isaiah 26:3).

I wrote the following poem for my dear friend Jerry O'Bryan, whose spirit is strong though his body is in a battle with Crohn's disease.

THE COST OF CHARACTER

- There is no mountain without a valley.
- There is no solution without a problem.
- There is no song without a sorrow.
- There is no dream without discontent.
- There is no strength without pain.
- There is no courage without fear.
- There is no victory without a battle.
- There is no success without sacrifice.
- There is no healing without a wound.
- There is no miracle without a need.
- There is no peace without a peril.
- There is no character without the anvil and the hammer.

GOD'S AMBUSH

And the LORD said to Moses, "Why do you cry to Me? Tell the children of Israel to go forward. But lift up your rod, and stretch out your hand over the sea and divide it. And the children of Israel shall go on dry ground through the midst of the sea."...Then Moses stretched out his hand over the sea; and the LORD caused the sea to go back by a strong east wind all that night, and made the sea into dry land, and the waters were divided. So the children of Israel went into the midst of the sea on the dry ground, and the waters were a wall to them on their right hand and on their left.

(Exodus 14:15–16, 21–22)

Storm clouds gathered as the voice of God began to sing the song of deliverance. The seas trembled and hid themselves. The foot of God was about to step on the oppressors of the Israelites. The desert sky was blackened with the arrival of God's war party. Lightning bolts hurtled like sparks from the wheels of God's chariots as they approached the battlefield, and God cleared a path for Moses and His children.

Pharaoh and his army raced thoughtlessly after the Israelites and into the opening that was once the sea. The storm overhead confused them. The dry ground beneath their feet made no sense. This was Pharaoh's appointment with God.

The Israelites were following the pillar through the sea to the other side. Once God saw that the Israelites were safe, He released the sea. Pharaoh's army was doomed. By the time the sea returned to its God-appointed home, the Egyptian army was dead.

CEMETERY IN THE SEA

At last, the past was behind the Israelites. The sea that brought death to the Egyptians brought life to the Israelites. When the sea returned, it separated them from Egypt. The footprints of yesterday were washed away. Not only did the army of Pharaoh die there, but slavery in Egypt died there as well. As always, God has the last word.

GETTING OUT OF THE PAST

PERSONAL EVALUATION

Read each of the following statements and answer **True** or **False**.

1. There are things in my past that hinder my personal growth.

2. Satan uses my past to haunt and accuse me.

3. I believe God can use the negative circumstances of my past as stepping-stones to promote me in my present and my future.

4. I have total peace concerning my past.

5. My past has made me skeptical of people.

6. My past has made me fearful.

7. I realize I need the help of a counselor to overcome certain circumstances of my past.

PERSONAL REFLECTION

Meditate on the following questions and answer them honestly.

1. Have I truly put the past behind me? *Not. Yet. But words*

2. What part of my past, if any, am I having trouble conquering? *My getty married the Second time*

3. Are there any stories I tell over and over about a certain incident that happened to me in my

childhood, hoping some listening ear will unlock the door of that mental prison for me?

4. Have I turned my past over to God yet? $\mathcal{C}$

GROUP DISCUSSION

1. Discuss what is meant by living life in the rearview mirror.

2. Could the journey through the Red Sea be considered a type of New Testament baptism? Explain.

3. Have one or two members of the group share personal testimonies of how they overcame their past.

4. Discuss God's advice to Moses in Exodus 14:13-14, when He told the Israelites to stand still, see God, and hold their peace. How does this relate to your situations today?

5. Discuss the poem titled "The Cost of Character" in this chapter.

GROUP EXERCISE

This exercise should be done at a pond, lake, river, stream, or other large body of water. You may wish to incorporate it into a group picnic or outing.

Have the individuals in the group recall the name of someone in their past whom they have had a difficult time forgiving. Have each person then write the name on a small sheet of paper. They may even wish to write about a particular incident. After this is finished (privately and confidentially), give each participant a small stone or rock about the size of a softball. Now have everyone tape the papers to the rocks.

At this point read the story of Israel's journey through the Red Sea in Exodus 14. At the end of the story, read from Philippians 3:

> *Not that I have already attained, or am already per-fected; but I press on, that I may lay hold of that for which Christ Jesus has also laid hold of me. Brethren, I do not count myself to have apprehended; but one thing I do, forgetting those things which are behind and reaching forward to those things which are ahead, I press toward the goal for the prize of the upward call of God in Christ Jesus.*
>
> (Philippians 3:12-14)

Now have each member of the group step forward, one at a time, and cast his or her stone into the deepest part of the water. As soon as this is done, have the group celebrate this victory by praising God together.

chapter 5

GETTING RID OF BITTERNESS

CAMPING AT MARAH AND ELIM

*So Moses brought Israel from the Red Sea; then they went
out into the Wilderness of Shur. And they went three days in
the wilderness and found no water. Now when they came to
Marah, they could not drink the waters of Marah, for they
were bitter. Therefore the name of it was called Marah. And
the people complained against Moses, saying, "What shall we
drink?" So he cried out to the LORD, and the LORD showed him
a tree. When he cast it into the waters, the waters were made
sweet. There He made a statute and an ordinance for them.
And there He tested them.* (Exodus 15:22–25)

Three days without water. Anger, muttering, and frustration—
these were the responses of the Israelites to their experiences
during their first week in the wilderness. Little did they
know that God would have them confront one of the enemies of
their souls at the camp of Marah. Their parched tongues revealed an
even greater fire within—a fire that burned deep in the reservoir of
their souls.

Even though their enemy was dead, the bitter memories of
Egyptian slavery were still very much alive in the active files of

their minds. God had removed them from their enemies, but now He had to remove the disease of slavery inflicted upon their souls.

At last they found a brook. The sound of tumbling waters invited them. Just as they cupped their hands to drink, someone cried, "Bitter water!" Enraged with fear, the people became desperate, for the contaminated water could not compare to the bitterness within the Israelites.

WHEN THE BETTER HALF BECOMES THE BITTER HALF

Bitterness! Nothing dries the taste buds like the sour taste of bitterness. Often, we react in the same way when someone's attitude has gone bitter.

> *Bitterness is a cancer of the soul. It eats away your spiritual life until your once vibrant testimony is in shambles.*

Mary Ruth and Claude (not their real names) were a typical couple who sat together on Sundays, ate at the dinner table with their four children, and played in the yard with the family dog. Their life appeared to be ideal. For the most part it was, with the exception of Claude's stressful job and Mary Ruth's obsession with worry and fear. These two problems culminated in a tense marital relationship. After fifteen years of marriage, Claude and Mary Ruth began to grow apart.

It wasn't long before Claude started talking to a lady at work about her troubles. Talking about this woman's problems made him feel useful, and his concern made her feel cared for. What began in innocence gradually turned into affection. Neither of them planned it, or even really wanted it, but it happened.

Soon Mary Ruth knew something was troubling Claude. In a matter of weeks, it all came out into the open. The next few days were filled with Mary Ruth's distrustful accusations, coupled with more fear. Eventually, Mary Ruth and Claude went to a family counselor to reconcile their relationship. Everything seemed to go well for a while, but Mary Ruth's suspicions gradually returned and grew worse. Her fear and worry escalated until she found herself in a deep emotional pit, out of control. When she finally filed for divorce, Claude begged her to reconsider. He genuinely apologized and fought desperately to save their marriage.

After the divorce, Claude moved out, and he remarried a few years later. His leaving, however, did not seem to help Mary Ruth's behavior. She became suspicious of other people and eventually isolated herself from society completely, as her fear and distrust continued. Claude and their children received healing through prayer and counseling. Time removed virtually all scars from their lives.

Mary Ruth, however, still lives with bitterness and distrust of everyone she meets.

How Bitterness Gets In

Hebrews 12:15 says, *"See to it that no one misses the grace of God and that no bitter root grows up to cause trouble and defile many"* (NIV).

Bitterness is a cancer of the soul. It eats away your spiritual life until your once vibrant testimony is in shambles. It spreads faster than the common cold and threatens the survival of ministries, churches, families, and individuals. This Scripture in Hebrews tells us that we must search our lives to see if any bitterness resides within. Note what it says: first it will trouble *you*, then *many* will be defiled.

Bitterness usually enters through a hurt. It makes no difference if the hurt was intentional or unintentional. Bitterness is conceived in the womb of an unresolved offense. It may be disguised as embarrassment, disappointment, or even ignorance.

The root of bitterness can be detected in our emotions. Like a stamp that can be seen only under an infrared light, our bitterness is revealed beneath the ray of emotions. The inner statements of the heart disclose the root of an embittered attitude. We justify its residency by reasoning that the "perpetrator" of the hurt hasn't paid enough for the wrong deed.

THE BITTER CONSEQUENCES

If only the "victim" could realize that bitterness wounds him or her far more deeply than the person who committed the wrong. It stifles self-esteem and hinders our walk with God. In Ephesians 4:31 we read, *"Let all bitterness, wrath, anger, clamor, and evil speaking be put away from you, with all malice."*

Bitterness usually enters through a hurt, intentional or unintentional, and is conceived in the womb of an unresolved offense.

This passage of Scripture explains how the *seed of bitterness* grows into sin. Again, it all begins with a hurt. That hurt turns to *wrath*, which is a seething inner feeling. Then it turns to *anger*, which occurs when the inner emotion is evident externally. Anger then graduates to *clamor*, which is foolish talking that comes from an angry soul. Clamor then turns to *evil speaking*. This is when we willfully say things designed to injure and hurt someone else. The last stage is *malice*, the intent to act to harm another person.

Health Consequences

People who become embittered put themselves at great risk for heart disease and strokes. Their blood pressure becomes abnormal, their respiratory systems are strained, their heart palpitations escalate, and they fall into the high-risk factor for stress-related physical ailments.

Social Consequences

In addition to the physical side effects, there are equally as many sociological side effects. Bitter people experience a great loss of social skills that can be traced to their highly suspicious natures. They greet the world in a defensive mode, thus spoiling relationships before they have a chance to flourish. Many bitter people find it difficult to make new friends, keep old friends, or ever have a close or best friend. The tendency is to live a life of alienation.

Spiritual Consequences

There are also spiritual side effects for bitter individuals. Prayer becomes difficult and is hindered because their thoughts are so embedded with doubt. Worship becomes mundane and routine because of a fear of openness and responsiveness. Faith becomes weak—almost impossible.

Psychological Consequences

The psychological fallout can be even worse. Bitter people see themselves as victims. Their defensive and suspicious behaviors often result in personality disorders. The risk of harboring bitterness is too great. It must be sought out, identified, and removed at the root.

UPROOTING BITTERNESS

The name *Marah* means "bitter." It wasn't mere chance that God led Israel to murky and poisoned waters. The people weren't really there to find the water, they were there to find the tree. In Exodus 15:25 we read, *"So he cried out to the LORD, and the LORD showed him a tree. When he cast it into the waters, the waters were made sweet."* As the bitter waters were made sweet through the observance of this unusual and unlikely process, *"there He* [God] *made a statute and an ordinance for them. And there He tested them"* (verse 25).

> ## God offered His name, Jehovah Rapha *(God Heals)*, as a guarantee that He would heal the bitterness in the people and would serve justice on the circumstances.

Why a tree? Perhaps this tree was a foreshadowing of the tree on which the Savior would hang many years later.

God offered His name, *Jehovah Rapha* (God Heals), as a guarantee that He would heal the bitterness in the people and would serve justice on the circumstances:

> *If you diligently heed the voice of the LORD your God and do what is right in His sight, give ear to His commandments and keep all His statutes, I will put none of the diseases on you which I have brought on the Egyptians. For I am the LORD who heals you* [Jehovah Rapha]. (Exodus 15:26)

There is only one cure for bitterness: forgiveness.

CAN I FORGIVE?

Getting out of the past involves the process of forgiveness. Forgiveness does not mean, "I set you free from the pain you caused me." It does not mean, "I will forget it and work never to let it happen again." Neither does it mean that the innocent absorb guilt, shame, and anger, while the guilty are let off the hook. It also does not mean that you decide to excuse the wrong that was done.

Forgiveness simply means this: I am relinquishing myself from the responsibility of bringing revenge on the person who did wrong. It means that I am turning this case over to a higher court—God's court—because His Word says, *"Vengeance is Mine, I will repay,' says the Lord"* (Romans 12:19). It also means that the perpetrator of my pain has the same opportunity that I did to find grace and forgiveness at the foot of the cross. *"If we confess our sins, He is faithful and just to forgive us our sins and to cleanse us from all unrighteousness"* (1 John 1:9). That forgiveness is available to everyone who humbly confesses to God—even those who have hurt me.

The process of forgiveness is twofold:

1. Decide never to bring up the offense *against* that person again. It may be brought up as a reference, but never as an accusation.

2. Believe that God's justice will decide whether to bring vengeance or mercy and forgiveness in due season.

In chapter 4, I related the story of Jackie. She continued her therapy for several months, always coming to a point of confrontation with her past and the perpetrator of her pain. As I led her closer to the moment of confrontation, she would say to me, "I can't forgive him for what he did."

The day finally came when I asked her to write out a contract of forgiveness. By this time she understood that she was not justifying the individuals who did her wrong or their actions; instead, she was releasing herself from the responsibility of bringing judgment against them. Her contract read something like this:

Dear_____,

After a long talk with God and my counselor, I have decided to forgive you.

I know what you did to me was wrong; however, I am leaving this matter in the hands of God. As of this day, [date], I will no longer be responsible for bringing judgment against you.

I forgive you and pray that you will find God in your life.

Jackie

A few weeks after this session, she wrote me a lengthy letter telling me how the power of forgiveness had totally changed her life. She even felt free enough to share her testimony a few months later, which prompted healing in the lives of others who had been abused.

Sometimes victims feel as though they have no future. Their hopelessness chains them to yesterday. This brings us to Ephesians 4:32: *"Be kind to one another, tenderhearted, forgiving one another, just as God in Christ forgave you."*

THE BETTER TRUTH

"Then they came to Elim, where there were twelve wells of water and seventy palm trees; so they camped there by the waters" (Exodus 15:27). After staying (and muttering) at Marah, they traveled six miles to *Elim*, meaning "strong trees," "palm trees," or "terebinths." Elim represents peace, the obvious place to overcome bitterness. The better (not bitter) truth is this: you don't have to stay at the camp of bitterness.

One Sunday morning I spoke on the subject of bitterness. I had two of our elders bring a large, rugged, seven-foot cross down the aisle and place it in front of the altar. I gave the other elders a hammer and a handful of nails. That morning, each person received a blank piece of paper. They were instructed to write the name of the person who had hurt them and to come and nail the paper to the cross. I have never seen more powerful deliverances in an altar response. The people stood in a line that stretched to the back of the building in order to get rid of their bitterness. That morning, those people discovered that peace was just a nail away, as illustrated in the chorus of one of my favorite hymns:

> *Forgiveness means that the perpetrator of my pain has the same opportunity that I did to find grace and forgiveness at the foot of the cross.*

Leave it there, leave it there,
Take your burden to the Lord
and leave it there;
If you trust and never doubt,
he will surely bring you out;
Take your burden to the Lord
and leave it there.

—C. Albert Tindley (1851–1933)

Yes for Give you John for all the Pain you cause me Through out all these Years Thank you Lord 9.8.2011

GETTING RID OF BITTERNESS

PERSONAL EVALUATION

Read each of the following statements and answer **True** or **False**.

1. I have dealt with all of the roots of bitterness in my life.

2. There is no one in my life I haven't forgiven.

3. I fully understand what it means to forgive someone.

4. I understand the physical, emotional, and spiritual dangers of harboring bitterness within.

5. I no longer hold myself responsible to bring justice to those who have wronged me. I realize that is God's job.

PERSONAL REFLECTION

Meditate on the following questions and answer them honestly.

1. Do I fully trust God to bring justice or mercy to those who have done me wrong?

2. Can I truly forgive inasmuch as I can decide never to bring up the offense *against* my perpetrator again?

3. Are there any hidden seeds of resentment or anger in my life that could eventually turn into bitterness?

4. Is there anyone I should go to and ask his or her forgiveness?

Group Discussion

1. Discuss the process of how anger and resentment can turn into bitterness.

2. Read and discuss Ephesians 4:31-32.

3. Read and discuss the power of forgiveness in Matthew 6:12-15.

4. Ask a member of the group to share a personal experience of forgiveness and the changes that followed.

5. Discuss the two-point process of forgiveness:

   • Decide never to bring up the offense against that person again. It may be brought up as a reference, but never as an accusation.

   • Believe that God will bring justice or mercy in due season.

6. Discuss the danger of always seeing yourself as a victim and viewing the world through the eyes of fear. Discuss how much better it is to view yourself as an overcomer.

7. Discuss the significance of the camp of Elim, which followed Marah. (See Exodus 15:27.)

GROUP EXERCISE

To do this exercise, you will need the following supplies: a small wooden cross, blank pieces of paper, pens or pencils, a hammer, and some small nails.

Have the members of the group write down the names of individuals they need to forgive. Have them come, one at a time, and nail the paper to the cross. A brief moment of worship should follow to allow the Holy Spirit time to confirm this act of forgiveness and to bring peace.

chapter 6

Getting Rid of Murmuring

Camping at the Wilderness of Sin and Rephidim

Do everything without complaining or arguing.
(Philippians 2:14 NIV)

And they journeyed from Elim, and all the congregation of the children of Israel came to the Wilderness of Sin, which is between Elim and Sinai, on the fifteenth day of the second month after they departed from the land of Egypt. Then the whole congregation of the children of Israel complained against Moses and Aaron in the wilderness. And the children of Israel said to them, "Oh, that we had died by the hand of the LORD in the land of Egypt, when we sat by the pots of meat and when we ate bread to the full! For you have brought us out into this wilderness to kill this whole assembly with hunger."
(Exodus 16:1–3)

The trip was set. Several of us would be traveling together to a convention. As a group, we had gone out for a meal several times but had never stayed together for any length of time. We decided to meet for breakfast to begin our day. Doug was one of the nicest guys you would ever want to meet—witty, considerate, and a good conversationalist. When we arrived for the meal, Doug and his wife, Marge (not their real names), were already there. We noticed that Marge was talking with one of the waiters about seating the group together. She seemed a little upset, but we thought she was just having a bad day. As soon as we were seated, she called for the waiter to bring a clean towel so we could reclean the table. No one really noticed the smudge, but she was greatly annoyed by it. She seemed to indicate that this was an ongoing problem for Doug and her, and they had boycotted many restaurants because of it.

> *When you choose your friends, choose them carefully. They will have either a positive or a negative influence on you.*

As the meal progressed, she refused the coffee and asked for a freshly brewed cup. She even had one of the chairs exchanged with one from another table because it was dusted with a few crumbs from a previous customer. Later, she sent her food back to be cooked longer and got upset with the waiter several times for delays. By the time we left the restaurant, she was miserable and declared that she would never go there again. I think she is still warning people of its perils. I believe we all hoped that her complaints were genuine and that the rest of the trip to the convention would be less eventful. We were not so fortunate.

Each restaurant we chose had at least three or four problems, each of which was treated as a major affront. Each hotel we stayed in had hard beds, cheap pillows, and rude service. She complained if there was a tinge of smoke, even in the hallways. We were careful not to exceed the speed limit, not to stop too frequently, not to see any tourist attractions along the way, and not to take too long to find a good hotel in the evening. Marge didn't enjoy any of the days of travel because riding in the car made her sick. She refused to tip any of the servers because of poor service and always filled out the complaint card at each hotel.

The rest of our party tried to ignore her responses, but we found ourselves catering to her whims in hopes of avoiding further complaints. Her constant complaining brought stress on the entire caravan. It goes without saying that many have declared that they will not travel with her again. You guessed it—she has complained about that, too.

Marge has been complaining for years, and will probably continue to do so. However, her complaining precipitated complaints among those of us who despise it. She complained about everything we did, and we all complained about her.

You become like the people who surround you. That is the power of influence. Ralph Waldo Emerson once said, "You become what you think about all day." If you choose to hang out with complainers, you may eventually become one yourself.

We are not responsible for the actions of a complainer; we are only responsible for our own actions. We must decide now that associating with complainers will have negative effects. I believe that you can determine what you will be like in five years by these three things:

- The books you read.
- The decisions you make.
- The people with whom you associate.

You cannot expect to be a positive person if all of your friends are negative. When you choose your friends, choose them carefully.

They will have either a positive or a negative influence on you. Discouraged people can change, but a person with a complaining spirit will not change until the problem is addressed through counseling or deliverance. Those with a complaining spirit need to see their problem as a disease of the soul described in 2 Thessalonians:

> *For we hear that there are some who walk among you in a disorderly manner, not working at all, but are busybodies....But as for you, brethren, do not grow weary in doing good. And if anyone does not obey our word in this epistle, note that person and **do not keep company with him**, that he may be ashamed.*
> (2 Thessalonians 3:11, 13–14, emphasis added)

However, the next verse is quick to add, *"Yet **do not count him as an enemy**, but admonish him as a brother"* (verse 15, emphasis added).

If you are besieged with someone with a complaining spirit, or if you recognize it within yourself, the first thing you can do is to start praying for the people with whom you surround yourself. Simply begin to pray this prayer:

> *Dear God, take all of the wrong people out of my life and put all of the right people in.*

BREAD, BIRDS, BROOKS, AND BUSYBODIES

Can God provide a table in the wilderness? Such a limited question is inappropriate when you are talking about the Creator of the universe. The only question is, *what* will He provide? This story about the Wilderness of Sin and Rephidim is told quite often from the pulpit. God sends manna, quail, and water from a rock. Amazing! While we are caught up in the unique nature of the miracles, we can forget the problem the miracles alleviated.

Miracles are not for entertainment. They are not to give men a career boost. Miracles are divine interventions in life designed to cause an effect that will bring about change. No miracle occurs without a greater purpose. The manna, quail, and water were all miracles, but they were sent only to cure the inner cancer of complaint.

The term *Wilderness of Sin* is not used in the same way the English word *sin* is used. It is simply the name of a place. It comes from the Hebrew word *Ciyn*, which is of uncertain derivation. *Rephidim*, however, means "the bottom." You might say that God views the spirit of complaining as *reaching the bottom*.

> *Miracles are divine interventions in life designed to cause an effect that will bring about change.*

Many people have asked me, "How did I get this way?" How does a mother change from being proud of her newborn to stifling the child with constant criticism? How does one go from being a trusted friend to a gossiping enemy? Going to the bottom doesn't occur in an instant. It is a downward process that starts with thinking the wrong thoughts and impulsively blurting them out loud. This creates a bad habit—the habit of complaining.

THE HABIT GOD HATES

Murmur comes from the Hebrew word *luwn*, which means "to stop," "stay permanently," or "to be obstinate." What a fixation. Complaining will cost you progress and growth. It will stop your maturing process until you cannot relate properly to others because your paradigm of the world has become bleak and hopeless.

I am not saying that one should never complain. I am not opposed to constructive criticism. God is not angry because we have an opinion. There are times when we use the method of complaint to speak up and correct wrong or unjust circumstances. However, the downward process of the Israelites began with their complaining against Moses (Exodus 16:2), which then led to complaining against God—both results of a lack of faith and trust in God.

The problem is not necessarily with the complaint; it is with the *habit* —a habit of complaining—that leads to the contamination of one's own character. The progressive steps down from a single complaint to the habit of complaining often take this spiritual detour:

1. Complaining about circumstances.
2. Complaining about people.
3. Complaining about those with authority who are in leadership.
4. Complaining against and distrusting God!

Notice what the Bible says about murmuring:

Also Moses said, "This shall be seen when the LORD gives you meat to eat in the evening, and in the morning bread to the full; for the LORD hears your complaints which you make against Him. And what are we? Your complaints are not against us but against the LORD."...Therefore the people contended with Moses, and said, "Give us water, that we may drink." And Moses said to them, "Why do you contend with me? Why do you tempt the LORD?"
(Exodus 16:8; 17:2)

A ROCK, A RIVER, AND A RIOT

The story continues. The complaining had now spread in epidemic proportions throughout the camp of the Israelites.

And the LORD said to Moses, "Go on before the people, and take with you some of the elders of Israel. Also take in your hand your rod with which you struck the river, and go. Behold, I will stand before you there on the rock in Horeb; and you shall strike the rock, and water will come out of it, that the people may drink." And Moses did so in the sight of the elders of Israel.

(Exodus 17:5–6)

God was showing them the cure for complaining, although they hadn't seen it yet. Notice what happened among the people when God tried to open the healing stream from the rock: *"So he [Moses] called the name of the place Massah and Meribah, because of the contention of the children of Israel, and because they tempted the LORD, saying, 'Is the LORD among us or not?'"* (verse 7).

WHEN GOD COMMANDS YOUR ATTENTION

The rock gave them water, but the miracle had no influence on their attitude. God wanted to give them the opportunity for change. In his book *The Winning Attitude*, John Maxwell writes, "Change comes one of three ways: (1) You will change when you hurt enough that you have to change. (2) You will change when you learn enough that you want to change. (3) You will change when you receive enough that you are able to change."

So it was that God had to become the schoolmaster who sent Israel, the pupil, to sit in the corner. The scenario abruptly changes and these terrifying words come crashing through the pages of Israel's history: *"Now Amalek came and fought with Israel in Rephidim"* (Exodus 17:8).

> *The problem is with the habit —the habit of complaining— that leads to the contamination of one's own character.*

85

Out of nowhere came war. A people who couldn't even follow the simple directions of their leader had lost faith in their God. They had become as disorganized as a newly disturbed anthill. Now, war was on their doorstep.

The Amalekites were descendants of Esau, and, of course, were ultimately from the seed of Abraham. This war was no national crisis; it was a family crisis. Notice how Israel responded to it. Although they were divided, this band of vagrants pulled together to face the crisis. Joshua sought cooperation from all of the tribes. (See verses 9–10.) Suddenly, all of the things they had been complaining about became insignificant.

DIAGNOSIS OF A COMPLAINER

A great therapy for complainers is for them to ask someone who loves them to secretly write down every time they complain, to log the complaints. Then, at the end of the week, they are to sit down and review the list. The discovery is amazing. They find that most of the time they do not have strong feelings about the complaints; complaining is merely an automatic reaction to a habitual negative thought process. If you were to put a complaint under a microscope, you would most likely see the following formula:

Inconvenience + Impulsive Speaking + Negative Thinking = Complaining

Complaining often ceases in a crisis because the individual becomes more focused on what is urgent. Not only is the inconvenience accepted, but consideration of others and their feelings often take precedence. Also, the focus becomes one of seeking a remedy for a negative situation—hoping and praying for a positive outcome. Arguments cease when a child is hurt or someone's life is in danger. Insignificant things fade into the background, and significant things surface. Most habitual complaining *is* trivial and meaningless. It only distracts our focus from the important things in life.

My daughter Brittany was in an accident in 1993. I was away on a hunting trip when a neighboring farmer brought me the news. That two-hour drive to the hospital seemed like an eternity. God had my attention. I was focused on all the right things—her safety, my love for her, my wife (who was there without me), and my other daughter, Lindsay. All of these were the things that I should have been focused on each day. My only response was, *Lord, I'm depending on You.*

> *Most habitual complaining is trivial and meaningless. It only distracts our focus from the important things in life.*

Rephidim was stained with blood from the warfare with the Amalekites. God forgives, but many times we have to contend with the consequences of our actions. It doesn't mean we aren't forgiven; it does mean that every decision has a consequence. Choose carefully.

THE HABIT GOD HEALS

Since much of the harm in a complaining spirit comes from the words we say, this is where healing must begin. It is not good enough to simply quit saying the *wrong things*. We must start saying the *right things*. The tool that was used as a weapon to tear down was originally created for praise and building up others. If you take off only the old man without putting on the new man, you are leaving the door open for the old man to return. You must close the door to the attitude of complaint by conforming to your original design—praise and encouragement. Learn to say the right things. Practice saying the right things. Develop a winning vocabulary and ask God to help you to become an encourager. Here are some positive and winning phrases you can use as you develop your winning vocabulary:

- "Have a great day."
- "I love you."
- "You are doing a good job."
- "You have such a good attitude."
- "You are so considerate."
- "Can I do anything to help you?"
- "I need you."
- "You are so talented."
- "Nothing is going to happen today that God and I can't handle."

A couple of years ago I was introduced to a simple little tool called "I like you because..." notes. Since then, I have used them religiously with my staff, friends, family, and public servants. The process is simple. Create a generic card that says, "I like [person's name] because [write compliment]."

Then sign your name. Here is an example:

I like _____ *John* _____

because *He is a good waiter and smiles all the time.*
He is very considerate to his customers.

Signed, _____

The positive effects of this simple tool are incredible. They not only make you feel better about yourself, but they also have such a positive impact on the recipients. Service improves, friendships blossom, respect levels rise, and, best of all, it's a great way to let your light shine.

PRACTICE ENCOURAGEMENT

And Moses said to Joshua, "Choose us some men and go out, fight with Amalek. Tomorrow I will stand on the top of the hill with the rod of God in my hand." So Joshua did as Moses said to him, and fought with Amalek. And Moses, Aaron, and Hur went up to the top of the hill. And so it was, when Moses held up his hand, that Israel prevailed; and when he let down his hand, Amalek prevailed. But Moses' hands became heavy; so they took a stone and put it under him, and he sat on it. And Aaron and Hur supported his hands, one on one side, and the other on the other side; and his hands were steady until the going down of the sun. So Joshua defeated Amalek and his people with the edge of the sword. Then the LORD said to Moses, "Write this for a memorial in the book and recount it in the hearing of Joshua, that I will utterly blot out the remembrance of Amalek from under heaven." And Moses built an altar and called its name, The-LORD-Is-My-Banner [Jehovah Nissi]; for he said, "Because the LORD has sworn: the LORD will have war with Amalek from generation to generation." (Exodus 17:9–16)

Encouragement is exemplified in this story. Moses lifted his rod and Israel prevailed against Amalek. When this eighty-year-old's arms got tired and dropped to his sides, Amalek prevailed. Here is where we really see the healing of the complaining spirit. Nothing conquers an ill feeling like the power of love. Moses stood

89

summoning the angels of heaven to fight with Israel, but his physical strength was failing. He leaned upon a rock (another symbol of Christ). Suddenly, as if the Master swept His brush across the canvas to complete a portrait, it all came together. Aaron, the priest, and Hur, the Levite, came to Moses' aid. Israel was losing. Moses was collapsing. Rephidim's valley was reeking with blood and the cries of war. The cattle were scattering. Chariots were overturning. Simultaneously, the priest grabbed one of Moses' hands, the Levite the other. Together, they raised Moses' arms toward the heavens. Now, there was unity and victory, and Amalek fled in defeat.

> *Disharmony turns to unity when we focus on Christ and others, and the ministry of encouragement is birthed.*

Disharmony turns to unity when we focus on Christ and others. The ministry of encouragement is birthed. *Jehovah Nissi* means "The Lord is my banner, or flag." You can talk about anyone you want, as long as the person you are talking to is God. Whose flag are you flying?

GETTING OUT OF THE HABIT OF COMPLAINING

PERSONAL EVALUATION

Read each of the following statements and answer **True** or **False**.

1. I do not have any friends who have the habit of complaining.
2. I am in the habit of complaining.
3. I believe that the habit of complaining is a sin.
4. I believe that complaining will hinder my spiritual journey.
5. I have a winning vocabulary.
6. I am a positive thinker.
7. I speak more compliments than I do complaints.
8. I am a very complimentary individual.
9. I surround myself with positive, well-balanced people.
10. I never complain about God and the way He operates.

PERSONAL REFLECTION

Meditate on the following questions and answer them honestly.

1. Do I have a close friend who will tell me if I complain too much?

2. Would I choose me to be one of my closest friends?

3. Am I in the habit of complimenting and looking for the good in people and things?

4. Can God speak to me easily, or does He have to *get my attention*?

5. Have I chosen positive mentors to help guide me through life?

GROUP DISCUSSION

1. Discuss the importance of choosing friends who are not complainers.

2. Discuss how a complaining spirit can spread like a disease among a group.

3. Discuss the kind of testimony a chronic complainer has to unbelievers.

4. Discuss how a habit of complaining will hinder your Christian growth process.

5. Discuss what it means to have a winning vocabulary.

6. Discuss John Maxwell's three statements on change:

   • You will change when you hurt enough that you have to change.

   • You will change when you learn enough that you want to change.

   • You will change when you receive enough that you are able to change.

7. Ask each person to describe how he or she feels after leaving the presence of a chronic complainer.

8. Discuss what kind of message a complaining spirit is sending to God.

GROUP EXERCISE

Before the class begins, make up several "I like you because..." cards. Give the members of the group these cards and ask them to fill them out and give them away before the next time the group meets. Begin the next session by giving testimonies of the impact this positive gesture had on the recipients.

chapter 7

GETTING RID OF DOUBT

CAMPING AT MOUNT SINAI

In the third month after the children of Israel had gone out of the land of Egypt, on the same day, they came to the Wilderness of Sinai. (Exodus 19:1)

Barbara (not her real name) was raised in the church. In fact, she was raised in several churches. Her church attendance was somewhat regular despite her family's instability. When things would begin to go badly, the family would just move on. Because of this, her father became more of a pastor to her than anyone else. Years passed and Barbara eventually married. She and her husband raised a beautiful family and attended church once or twice a month.

One day my phone rang at six in the morning. On the other end, Barbara was sobbing as though her world had come to an end. Through her tears she asked, "How could God let these things keep happening to me?"

I prayed with her and asked her to meet me at my office later that day. As I began to probe into her knowledge of God, I found a lady who had an extremely distorted view of Him. Her relationship with God was built on fear rather than love. Her view of God was that of a dictatorial landlord. In the hour when she really needed God, she doubted His love, His care for her, and even His existence.

Barbara is typical of many who go to church but never truly go to God. They sing His songs but do not understand what they are singing. They are religious but not spiritual. They have a moderate level of commitment to the church, but they do not have a personal relationship with God. The creature and the Creator have never really communed. Worship, therefore, becomes an inconsequential duty and sermons have little impact.

Barbara's problem was doubt. Contrary to what it might seem, the opposite of doubt is not belief—it's trust. You can trust only when you truly know an individual. With trust comes faith. When we have faith, we no longer doubt. Scripture says,

> *Without faith it is impossible to please Him, for he who comes to God must believe that He is, and that He is a rewarder of those who diligently seek Him.*   (Hebrews 11:6)

A VISIT FROM GOD

Three months had passed since the Israelites had left Egypt. At Mount Sinai they set up camp for the next eleven months and five days. This was the place where Moses had been visited by God in a burning bush months earlier. (See Exodus 3.)

Sinai was a mountainous region, and Horeb was the name of one particular mountain in that region. There, God instructed Moses to draw a boundary line around the mountain base. Any person or animal setting foot upon the mountain would die. (See Exodus 19:12–13.) The people were instructed to wash themselves in order to *"be ready"* (verse 11) for God to descend upon the mountain on the third day. The anticipated third day came with a display that would make our most ornate fireworks seem like small candle flames in comparison.

A thick cloud rested on the mountain. From the cloud came a pompous fanfare of thunder accompanied by an array of lightning bolts as God *"descended upon it in fire"* (verse 18). All of this was accompanied by an overture of trumpet blasts. (See verse 16.) Smoke billowed skyward and the mountain shook profusely as God began to speak audibly to the company of Israelites. The people listened fearfully to the hallowed oration.

Contrary to what it might seem, the opposite of doubt is not belief—it's trust. You can trust only when you truly know an individual.

Afterward, they pleaded with Moses to speak for them because the scene was too frightening and they feared they would die if they heard from God directly. (See Exodus 20:19.) So, Moses agreed to approach the cloud alone.

Moses remained on the mountain with God for forty days. At some time during this period, God inscribed the Ten Commandments on two tablets of stone. On the fortieth day, God told Moses,

> *Go, get down! For your people whom you brought out of the land of Egypt have corrupted themselves. They have turned aside quickly out of the way which I commanded them. They have made themselves a molded calf, and worshipped it and sacrificed to it.* (Exodus 32:7–8)

The Israelites had done this because the people couldn't see Moses and presumed he had died. They could see God on the mountain, but they couldn't see Moses. The truth was that they looked to Moses as their leader rather than to God. Moses had, in essence, become their god. Their inability to see Moses prompted them to create yet another god to worship.

HOW DOUBT GETS INTO OUR SPIRIT

There are several ways in which our spirits can be corrupted by doubt.

1. Fixing Our Eyes on Man instead of on God

Man is certainly the representative of God, but he is never a substitute for God.

A few years ago a lady came to my office declaring that she was leaving the church and forsaking Christianity. She was convinced that all Christians were hypocrites and all ministers were liars. She continued to fume about churches being more concerned about money than they were about people.

> When you take your eyes off the destination, all you can see are your present surroundings.

After she vented her anger, she began to cry. Her real problem was that her favorite evangelist had been exposed as a moral failure. His crisis had capsized her faith. She eventually saw that he was only an imperfect man and concluded that she had placed him on a pedestal, yet she had never really prayed for him. She had taken so much from his ministry and never stopped to think what he needed from his followers to maintain his own level of faith. The tug of the crowd had finally become too hard for him. She had to realize that God had not failed; she had put her faith in a man who had failed.

2. Fixing Our Eyes on Our Circumstances instead of on God

All the Israelites could see was the present. God had them in the wilderness for a purpose. He never intended for them to remain there, but they took their eyes off the goal—Canaan. When you take your eyes off the destination, all you can see are your present surroundings.

We all have bad days, but that doesn't mean we have to succumb to having bad lives. I have a saying that I use around the office when things aren't going well: "It's only a day; it's not a life." We must become removed from our circumstances and emotions in order to accurately assess the situation.

3. Becoming Self-Centered instead of God-Centered

Life just doesn't seem to move fast enough for most of us. It is easy to get so locked in to our own philosophies and goals that we forget God's agenda.

We have always been torn between the will of God and our own will. We need to find the place where our wills and God's will become one. God has given man free will to choose the direction of his life. Many mistakenly believe that God's will is a burden to bear—an albatross around one's neck.

The key to God's will is found in the talents and interests He places within us. His will is not a magnetic force vying for our time and energies. The struggle of man is not with the will of God but rather with the desires of the flesh. Finding God's will thrusts us toward life's fullest capabilities and potentials.

4. Surrounding Ourselves with Doubters

Aaron and the elders had accompanied Moses on his initial journey on the mountain with God. It was easy to have faith while being surrounded by others who were seeing the same things. For Moses' forty-day visit with God, Aaron remained behind, where he became influenced by the doubters. His faith was replaced by discouragement when he wasn't on the mountain.

Today we can't always be on the mountain. It is our responsibility to remember in the dark those things that God told us in the light.

Doubters are threatened by anyone who has vision and faith. Every group has at least one doubter—probably more. Doubters come in all sizes and ages, but their mission is the same: to convince you of the many reasons why something can't be done. Doubters seem to have detectors for all the things that *might* go wrong. They may call themselves realists or conservatives, but the truth is that *"The just shall live by faith"* (Romans 1:17) is a foreign concept to them.

Doubters seem to know all the people who have tried and failed. They are prophets of doom. Their focus is singular, their dreams are limited, their risks are few, their faith is futile, and their fate is inevitable.

Faith vs. Doubt

Faith is always part of the answer;
Doubt is always part of the problem.

Faith always has a program;
Doubt always has an excuse.

Faith always says, "Let me do it for you";
Doubt says, "You're doing it wrong."

Faith sees an answer for every problem;
Doubt sees a problem for every answer.

Faith sees a green near every sandtrap;
Doubt sees two or three sandtraps near every green.

Faith says, "It may be difficult, but it's possible";
Doubt says, "It may be possible, but it's too difficult."

Walk by faith!

—Author unknown

THE QUEST TO SEE GOD

How often do you hear people say, "When I see it, I'll believe it"? What a pessimistic and immature statement. These people are basically saying to God, "Show it to me and I may believe."

God, on the other hand, says, "Believe and I'll show it to you."

The disease of doubt can only be cured by doses of *trust* and *faith*. Before trust is possible, a personal relationship with God must exist. We must see God for ourselves in order to trust and believe Him. Faith is a by-product of trusting God. The following three steps will help us to begin our own personal journeys with God.

> *We must see and know God for ourselves in order to trust and believe Him. Faith is a by-product of trusting God.*

1. We Need to Understand How God Thinks

God's thoughts are written in His Word. It is extremely important for us to own a version of the Bible that we can understand. God cannot speak to us if we don't understand what He is saying.

101

2. We Need to Communicate with God

This is done through prayer and meditation. Prayer should be comfortable and consistent. I suggest you block out time each morning to spend with God. Having praise choruses or slow, sacred music in the background creates an atmosphere for prayer.

Begin by thanking Him for all His blessings in your life. You will be surprised how it will bring you into a positive frame of mind before you start the day. I suggest you write down your prayer requests and either read the list or remind yourself that God knows your needs before you ask Him. Spend most of your time in prayer getting to know God.

After a time of thanking Him, you may wish to worship. Many people do not understand the difference between *praise* and *worship*. The terms are not synonymous.

Praise is thanking God for *what He has done.*

Worship is honoring and valuing God for *who He is.*

Scripture reminds us,

Do not be rash with your mouth, and let not your heart utter anything hastily before God. For God is in heaven, and you on earth; therefore let your words be few. (Ecclesiastes 5:2)

That means we should listen to Him more than we speak to Him. The author of that statement, Solomon, suggested that we should stand in awe of God and not be hasty with our words.

When we spend time with God, our minds may have the tendency to wander, perhaps organizing the activities of our day. Having a pen and pad nearby will usually remedy this hindrance. When a thought comes to you, write it down and return to your worship.

3. We Need to Serve God

"Those who wait on the LORD *shall renew their strength"* (Isaiah 40:31). The word *"wait"* in this passage has the connotation of a *waiter* or *waitress*. It implies that we serve while waiting for God. This is accomplished by doing things for others in the name of God. When we do things for the underprivileged, we are doing things for the Lord. (See Matthew 25:40.)

THE TOUCH OF HIS HAND—DOUBT IS GONE!

The disobedience of the Israelites brought discouragement to Moses. In a tent, outside the Hebrew camp, Moses privately communed with God. Then God led him to stand upon a rock, and told him, *"I...will cover you with My hand while I pass by"* (Exodus 33:22). What an amazing place to be, covered by God's hand. His touch protects us, reminds us of His mighty power, and is able to remove our doubt.

God's touch protects us, reminds us of His mighty power, and is able to remove our doubt.

Counseling is a wonderful tool, but it is limited without the touch of God. Preaching can be stimulating, but preaching alone cannot change a life without the touch of God. A song is not a psalm unless the touch of God is on it. A lesson is not a teaching unless it has the touch of God. A sermon is not a message without the touch of God.

This is not a carnal journey but a spiritual one. Our spirits are reaching for the Source from which they came. It is not a question of God's passing by. Rather, it is a question of our reaching out to touch Him. His presence fills the universe. One touch, and doubt dissipates. But be prepared—your spirit will long to touch Him time and time again. You will long to get away and sit in the cleft of the rock, to see Him with your spiritual eyes and feel Him brush by you in all of His glory. If doubt returns, go back to the rock and touch Him again. He'll be waiting.

ERADICATING DOUBT

PERSONAL EVALUATION

Read each of the following statements and answer **True** or **False**.

1. I sometimes doubt the existence of God.

2. I have a personal relationship with God.

3. I do not hold God responsible for the failures and mistakes of mankind.

4. I have not surrounded myself with doubters.

5. I have regular and meaningful communication with God.

6. I am a faithful worker in the kingdom of God.

7. I live by faith.

PERSONAL REFLECTION

Meditate on the following questions and answer them honestly.

1. Am I more convinced of the existence of Satan than I am of the existence of God?

2. Do I see God properly?

3. Have I allowed myself to become discouraged by the failures and mistakes of men and women who represent God?

4. Do I consider myself to be a good example of a Christlike person?

5. Am I out of focus in any area of my Christian walk?

GROUP DISCUSSION

1. Discuss the case study of Barbara at the beginning of this chapter. Ask the group to analyze how Barbara could stay in church for so many years and know so little about the Bible and God.

2. Read and discuss Hebrews 11:6 as it relates to believing in the existence of God.

3. Discuss the setting of Mount Sinai in Exodus 19 and try to determine why the people made the golden calf after witnessing such an awesome sight.

4. Discuss these four statements relating to how doubt gets into our spirits:

   • We take our eyes off God and place them on man.

   • We set our eyes on circumstances instead of on God.

   • We tend to be self-centered instead of God-centered.

   • We surround ourselves with doubters.

5. Discuss the poem "Faith vs. Doubt."

6. Have a member of the group relate a personal

experience about doubt and tell how he or she overcame it.

GROUP EXERCISE

Have the members of the group describe how they see God. This will be a powerful, faith-building exercise that will stimulate the minds and spirits of those who participate. During each person's description, ask the other members of the group to close their eyes so they may fully concentrate and get the impact of the exercise.

chapter 8

GETTING RID OF STRESS

CAMPING AT TABERAH, KIBROTH-HATTAAVAH, AND HAZEROTH

Now when the people complained, it displeased the LORD; for the LORD heard it, and His anger was aroused. So the fire of the LORD burned among them, and consumed some in the outskirts of the camp. Then the people cried out to Moses, and when Moses prayed to the LORD, the fire was quenched. So he called the name of the place Taberah, because the fire of the LORD had burned among them. (Numbers 11:1–3)

I remember coming into the house as a young boy and hearing the sound of the old pressure cooker. It was a large pot with a tightly fitted lid. When the pot heated up, pressure built up inside, thus providing energy to cook the food. On top was an apparatus we called the "sizzler." The job of the sizzler was to keep the pressure from building up too high, which would cause the pot to explode.

Stress builds up in our lives in the very same way that pressure builds in a cooker. If the sizzler ever failed, the pot would explode. Similarly, an overload of stress leads to burnout. The following are symptoms of stress, as well as some of the early stages of burnout:

- Constant dissatisfaction
- Restlessness
- Persistent fatigue
- Irritability (short fuse)
- Memory lapse
- Frustration with the progress of life

The phrase *stressed out* may be described in this way: "the emotional well has run dry, the physical motor is out of oil, and spiritual strength is depleted." Emotional downers create a syndrome of self-criticism, self-doubt, and self-pity. Spiritually, we begin to question God, discount His will, reject His Word, and refuse to utilize His resources.

> *Stress overload keeps us from focusing properly on life and on God, robbing us of our benevolent nature and replacing it with self-centeredness.*

Stress overload keeps us from focusing properly on life and on God. It robs us of our benevolent nature and replaces it with self-centeredness. With our focus on ourselves, we become easily offended and have a tendency to read the wrong message into circumstances.

Stress can cause you to walk through life with blinders on. Recently I read that horses have the largest eyes of any animal except the ostrich. Their eyes are located on the sides of their heads, permitting them to see in two different directions at once. However, they have a hard time seeing in front of their bodies. This is their blind spot. So it is with the stressed-out individual who is focused on the side issues but is blinded to the things right in front.

As I mentioned earlier, my friend Jerry O'Bryan was diagnosed several years ago with Crohn's disease. This incurable disease caused attachments like a spider's web to form inside his body between his internal organs. Once attached, the straw-like channels allow secretions to escape from one vital organ and flow into another. Treatment for this disease is complicated because it is not localized.

Stress moves through the spirit of man in much the same way that Crohn's disease moves through a body—entangling itself with our faith and other spiritual faculties. Because of too much stress, our spiritual vision may become distorted and our sensitivity to the leading of God calloused.

BURNED OUT BUT STILL BORN AGAIN

The stress of life can drain the energy out of many great leaders whose days are filled with long hours of ministry. Because of the busy schedule, the many complaints, and the heavy problems ministers encounter, burnout accelerates. It is easy to forget who the real audience is. Our audience is not people; our audience is God. We are not the stars; Jesus is the star. All we do is operate the spotlight.

Moses learned that leadership without delegation produces bottlenecks. He was feeling the effects of burnout when God told him to choose seventy elders to help oversee the people. God told Moses that He would come down in a cloud and *"take of the Spirit that is upon you and...put the same upon them"* (Numbers 11:17). The Spirit that was on Moses—the weight of ministry and the ability of God to meet that responsibility—was placed upon each of the elders. Scripture says that *"when the Spirit rested upon them* [the elders], *that they prophesied, although they never did so again"* (Numbers 11:25).

STRESS IN LEADERSHIP

Leadership is a breeding ground for jealousy and competition unless you are promoted through the ranks of "followship" first. Two men by the names of Eldad and Medad were prophesying in the camp instead of at the Tabernacle. A young man came to Moses complaining because that wasn't the way they always did it. Just as some forget the difference between organization and formalization, this young man was missing the point. He thought they were supposed to be "religious." Even Joshua urged Moses to make them stop. Moses refused, saying, *"Oh, that all the Lord's people were prophets and that the LORD would put His Spirit upon them!"* (Numbers 11:29).

> **Lead by example, and let your followers come after you. Titles mean nothing if you are not doing the job.**

Being different does not necessarily mean you are wrong. Many are judged for doing things in a different fashion. God chose to use John the Baptist, a wild, unshaven hermit. He also chose the hotheaded Peter, who denied Him. He chose a harlot in the city of Jericho to help the Israelites and a disobedient prophet named Jonah to go to Nineveh. God often uses the ordinary to do the extraordinary. God uses the ridiculous to perform the miraculous. God has always used *"the foolish things of the world to put to shame the wise, and God has chosen the weak things of the world to put to shame the things which are mighty"* (1 Corinthians 1:27). God knows all too well that critics of leaders are found in every arena.

In addition to handling the complaints of the people, Moses also dealt with jealousy from his own brother and sister. Aaron and Miriam complained, saying, *"Has the LORD indeed spoken only through Moses? Has He not spoken through us also?"* (Numbers 12:2). They were bickering, in a sense, over titles. They were jealous of Moses' position with God. *"So the anger of the LORD was aroused against them, and He departed. And when the cloud departed from above the tabernacle, suddenly Miriam became leprous"* (verses 9–10). Moses interceded for her, and God healed her, but not until she had been put out of the camp for seven days.

In *Developing the Leader Within You,* John Maxwell writes, "Leadership is not a position, it is influence." Don't demand respect and followership simply because of your position. Lead by example, and let your followers come after you. Titles mean nothing if you are not doing the job.

It doesn't matter what you are called as long as you are doing the job. Jealousy is a killer. Don't fall into this trap. It will rob you of friendships, influence, and your personal testimony.

BEATING BURNOUT AND STAMPING OUT STRESS

Here is a formula for beating stress:

1. Build your body.
2. Manage your mind.
3. Stabilize your self.
4. Assess your gifts.
5. Relish your relationships.
6. Balance your behavior.

Build Your Body

First, we must build our bodies, realizing that they are the epitome of God's physical creation. To abuse our bodies is to discredit the creation of God. To care for and build up our bodies is to present them unto the Lord as worship. Regular exercise is a vital weapon for controlling stress. "Breaking a sweat on a regular basis through meaningful, and hopefully enjoyable, exercise lowers the anxiety level and clears the mind," states Dr. Paul L. Walker. As we ask God to remove our stresses, we must realize that it is our responsibility to get our bodies in shape.

Manage Your Mind

Some people are stressed because they listen to the wrong people and the wrong things. So much of their stress could be alleviated by eliminating the time spent on the phone with negative people and by carefully choosing the things they read. Be selective and make sure that a proper dosage of the *right* stuff is going into your mind every day. A good question to ask is this: *What kind of positive information do I feed my mind each day, and is it enough to balance all the negative information I will hear?*

Stabilize Your Self

One of our greatest problems with stress is that we put more pressure on ourselves than we should. We have a big "image" problem in our country, worrying about what others think and say about us.

Here is a fun therapy to help you discover a little more about yourself. It is a simple, old-fashioned, image-association test.

1. Think of a color. Write down three words that describe that color.
2. Next, write down the name of your favorite animal. Write down three words that describe that animal.

The first set of three words describes how you truly are on the inside. The second set of three words describes how you would like others to view you. Subconsciously, we choose colors and animals that we can relate to. There is something about those choices that reveals a part of the inward self.

It is important to understand your strengths and weaknesses, as well as your temperament. Knowing these things about yourself will enable you to lead a less stressful life.

Assess Your Gifts

One thing the clergy has had to deal with in the last decade is the question of professionalism. We were told to break out of the country-preacher mode to become more equipped to teach and to hone our administrative skills. Now, many find themselves asking these questions: *Are we counselors or preachers? Administrators or shepherds? Businessmen or teachers?*

Knowing your strengths and weaknesses, as well as your temperament, will enable you to lead a less stressful life.

Unfortunately, the demand is that we be all of the above. I attended a pastors' conference last year where a layman spoke on what the laity wanted from their pastors. He listed the following things:

1. Administrator
2. Businessman
3. Marketer
4. Public relations expert
5. Psychologist/counselor
6. Master of ceremonies
7. Accountant

8. Building contractor

9. Balanced example of physical fitness

10. Family person

11. Spiritual leader

12. One who shows high accountability on all levels of job performance

13. Personal developer of all ministries

14. One who shares the responsibilities of laymen

He continued by saying, "I expect my pastor to pray every day; be respectful, supportive, and on-call when I need him. I expect him to have a vast knowledge of God's Word, to love, and to give of his time and finances." He concluded, "He must be a learner, advance to higher levels of learning, and work for reasonable pay." I was surprised that he didn't include "more powerful than a locomotive, faster than a speeding bullet, and able to leap tall buildings at a single bound"!

Obviously, one of our problems with stress is that we think we have to be great at everything. My advice is to know your limitations, delegate your weaknesses, and work within the parameters of your strengths. Relax.

Relish Your Relationships

Some stress is caused by never appreciating the value and talents of those around us. Instead, we try to fill a void by chasing ghosts of our every whim and fancy. Learn what are the truly valuable things in life, and learn to cut out those things that are insignificant.

- Learn the value of God—keep Him near you always.

- Learn the value of family—never take it for granted.

- Learn the value of marriage—never abuse it.

- Learn the value of children—take time to laugh and play with them.

- Learn the value of friends—pursue time together.

- Learn the value of purity—make it a personal goal.

- Learn the value of pleasures—they were put here for a purpose.

Stress is increased when we fail to draw strength from others. People are blessings. The truth is, no one has to like you, but the people who do like you choose to do so of their own free will. Cherish them.

Balance Your Behavior

Wrong behavior causes guilt, not release! Right behavior is a choice before it is a habit. It doesn't matter who is right, it is *what is right* that counts. We must make the choice to think the right thoughts. Right thoughts produce right actions, not the other way around. A balanced behavior is one that is not overdone in any one area. It reflects an attitude that is flexible and surrendered to the work and person of the Holy Spirit—a behavior distinctly different from those committed to this world's system. A balanced individual exemplifies the fruit of the Spirit, denoting that God is in control. A balanced behavior begins with the choice of right behavior, right thinking, and a right relationship with God.

GETTING RID OF STRESS

PERSONAL EVALUATION

Read each of the following statements and answer **True** or **False**.

1. I have a problem managing stress.
2. I take the complaints of others too personally.
3. I get the proper amount of exercise.
4. I draw strength from my relationship with my family.
5. My thoughts dwell more on the positive than the negative.
6. I like who I am and do not feel like I have an image problem.
7. I properly manage the things my mind feeds on.
8. I pray for temperance and patience.
9. I feel that I live my life in balance.
10. I have a positive friend I can call when I feel stressed out.
11. I feel that I realize the value of God in my life and keep Him near me always.

PERSONAL REFLECTION

Meditate on the following questions and answer them honestly.

1. Do I have my priorities in order concerning my relationships with family and friends?

2. Do I expect too much of myself and others?

3. Do I let little things get to me?

4. Do I take good care of my body?

5. Do I know who the audience is?

GROUP DISCUSSION

1. Discuss the importance of living a balanced life.

2. Discuss creative and practical ways to do the following things:

   - Build your body.

   - Manage your mind.

   - Stabilize yourself.

   - Assess your gifts.

   - Relish your relationships.

   - Balance your behavior.

3. Ask a member of the group to share a personal experience of being overstressed and to give a report of how he or she overcame it.

GROUP EXERCISE

Have the members of the group stand and form a single line. Next, have them place their hands on the shoulders of the person in front of them. Ask them to massage their neck and shoulders. Have them then turn and face the opposite direction and do the same thing.

This exercise will be fun as well as relaxing. You may even wish to conclude with an invigorating group walk around the block to really put into action the things you have studied.

chapter 9

GETTING RID OF FEAR

CAMPING AT KADESH BARNEA

And the LORD spoke to Moses, saying, "Send men to spy out the land of Canaan, which I am giving to the children of Israel; from each tribe of their fathers you shall send a man, every one a leader among them." So Moses sent them from the Wilderness of Paran according to the command of the LORD, all of them men who were heads of the children of Israel....Then Moses sent them to spy out the land of Canaan, and said to them, "Go up this way into the South, and go up to the mountains, and see what the land is like: whether the people who dwell in it are strong or weak, few or many; whether the land they dwell in is good or bad; whether the cities they inhabit are like camps or strongholds; whether the land is rich or poor; and whether there are forests there or not. Be of good courage. And bring some of the fruit of the land." Now the time was the season of the first ripe grapes.... Then they came to the Valley of Eshcol, and there cut down a branch with one cluster of grapes; they carried it between two of them on a pole. They also brought some of the pomegranates and figs....And they returned from spying out the land after forty days. Now they departed and came back to Moses and Aaron

*and all the congregation of the children of Israel in the Wilder-
ness of Paran, at Kadesh; they brought back word to them and to
all the congregation, and showed them the fruit of the land.*

(Numbers 13:1–3, 17–20, 23, 25–26)

F eel the wind in your face, the spring in your heels, and the
taste of triumph on your lips. This is the feeling you get seconds before crossing the finish line. Victory sings the praises of
a job well done, a long-awaited medallion, and the thrill of the conquest. Perhaps those few seconds on the edge make up for the years
of training and scores of sacrifices for which there are no records,
only scars.

"No pain, no gain," we keep saying. So we press on, knowing that
victory is achievable. The legendary football coach Vince Lombardi said,
"It's not whether you get knocked down, it's whether you get up." Success is getting back up one more time than you get knocked down. It's
the edge of victory that keeps us in the race when we feel like quitting.

Rabbi Zadok Rabinowitz wrote, "A man's dreams are an index
to his greatness." It is his dreams that make him feel alive. Author
Basil S. Walsh wrote, "If you don't know where you are going, how
can you expect to get there?" Many people are getting nowhere in
life simply because they aren't headed toward any specific place.

At last, the Promised Land was in sight. The mountains of
Hebron and the Valley of Eshcol looked magnificent. These wan-
derers were almost home. Their faces were dry and ruddy from the
year and a half of desert living. Their mouths watered for the familiar taste of herbs, garlic, and leeks. Their menu of manna, quail, and
occasional food from the land was getting old. Children dreamed of
playing in the pools of Gibeon and Heshbon. The aged could finally
rest by sitting in the shade of the poplars and enjoying the taste of
ripe olives, figs, and fresh bread. The women visualized new grains

and oils for baking. The men thought of rich land for planting and harvesting.

The nights now ended with the excited chatter of children who had high hopes of a land of milk and honey. For the moment, complaining had ceased and hope filled the hearts of the eager travelers. At last, the long period of testing would be over. The only thing left was to pass God's final exam.

MIRACLES AND FAITH

Many people assume that if God showed them a miracle, it would change their lives forever. But miracles do not produce faith; faith produces miracles.

The children of Israel saw the Red Sea part, manna fall from heaven, water flow from a rock, millions of quail be delivered by the wind, people experience healings of all sorts, and clothes and sandals never wear out. They heard God's audible voice, saw His presence each day in the pillar of cloud and fire, and witnessed His presence on the mountain with Moses and the seventy elders. They saw the plagues afflict Egypt and witnessed God's defeat of the Amalekites. All of this happened in just eighteen months. Surely they must have had incredible faith in the abilities and faithfulness of God. What could possibly hinder this kind of faith?

> *The greatest hindrance to the Israelites' faith, and to our faith today, is a four-letter word:* fear.

The greatest hindrance to faith is not the absence of God's power. The greatest hindrance to the Israelites' faith, and to our faith today, is a four-letter word: *fear.*

- Faith is the force that activates God's power in our lives.
- Fear is the force that activates Satan's power in our lives.

THE GRASSHOPPER SYNDROME

At God's command, Moses chose a man from each of the twelve tribes to send into the Promised Land as a spy. (See Numbers 13:3–16.) The spies covered the territory from Kadesh at the southern tip of the Desert of Zin, to Rehob at the northern tip, and back again (a round trip of approximately 500 miles). Anticipation was running high throughout the camp. They stood on the threshold of promise or peril.

Children ran through the camp proclaiming the news that the twelve spies were back from their mission. At the sound of the *shofar*, a ceremonial horn, the people gathered to hear the report. You could hear a pin drop as the spies testified to the richness of the land. They even brought clusters of grapes that took two men to carry. The land was everything God had promised.

While on the journey, however, they had seen men of great stature. Their hearts were pricked with fear. Most of the spies proclaimed, *"We are not able to go up against the people, for they are stronger than we....We were like grasshoppers in our own sight, and so we were in their sight"* (Numbers 13:31, 33). Scripture does not say that the giants called them grasshoppers. This is what they called themselves. Fear caused them to see themselves as inferior.

Two of the spies, however—Joshua and Caleb—perceived things quite differently: they were confident and determined.

- Ten came back complaining, and two came back conquering.
- Ten came back grumbling, and two came back gratified.

- Ten came back chiding, and two came back challenged.

- Ten came back horrified, and two came back hopeful.

- Ten came back oppressed, and two came back overcomers.

THE REVELATION OF CHARACTER

The way you see yourself determines the level of fear or faith that can operate in your life. These eighteen months in the desert were not to show them who God was; it was to show them who they were. God wanted to get them to stop thinking like slaves.

The purpose of the wilderness training camp was to reveal character. Famous basketball coach John Wooden wrote, "Be more concerned with your character than your reputation. Your character is what you really are, while your reputation is merely what others think you are."

> *The trials of life are there to bring out our latent qualities, not to fill us with the fear of defeat.*

The trials of life are there to bring out our latent qualities, not to fill us with the fear of defeat. Imagine 2.5 million people eating angel-baked bread and God-delivered quail and drinking miracle water, yet still feeling like grasshoppers. Before conquering the enemy, the supposed source of your fear, you must first conquer the real enemy: yourself.

THE REMEDY FOR FEAR IS COURAGE

Fear refines courage, and courage takes us across the finish line. Being afraid does not mean we are going to lose. A popular slogan on the back of sports attire proclaims, "No Fear." To approach life without any fear is to live in denial. The goal is to approach life with the assurance that we can conquer our fears. World War I flying ace Eddie Rickenbacker wrote, "Courage is doing what you're afraid to do. There can be no courage unless you're scared."

Similarly, Mark Twain once said, "Courage is resistance to fear and mastery of fear—not absence of fear." Fear tries to keep us from even trying.

THE BATTLE OF THE GIANTS

Before you can understand the faith of Joshua and Caleb, you must know that they too were "giants." In a physical sense, a giant is simply a man with an oversized body. However, the body is only part of a man. The whole person consists of a body, soul, and spirit. You can be a physical giant and a spiritual dwarf. In the case of Joshua and Caleb, however, they were spiritual giants.

As each of the spies gave his report, the people began to squirm. Their faith was shrinking. They could feel fear swelling. It began with a chatter; then, one negative statement bred another. Mothers clinched their children tighter each time one of the spies repeated the word *giant*. Old men looked to the ground in despair. The commotion heightened to a roar as the negativism spread through the tribes. They whispered at first, then shouted,

If only we had died in the land of Egypt! Or if only we had died in this wilderness! Why has the LORD brought us to this land to fall by the sword, that our wives and children should become victims? Would it not be better for us to return to Egypt?...Let us select a leader and return to Egypt. (Numbers 14:2–4)

Joshua and Caleb stood before the people and ripped their clothes. They referred to the cities waiting for them and that the "giants" would be "toast."

If the LORD delights in us, then He will bring us into this land and give it to us, "a land which flows with milk and honey." Only do not rebel against the LORD, nor fear the people of the land, for they are our bread; their protection has departed from them, and the LORD is with us. Do not fear them.

(Numbers 14:8–9)

They urged the people to trust God and not to fear, but their pleas went unheeded.

YOUR PROBLEM IS NOT YOUR PROBLEM

John Maxwell, in his book *Be All You Can Be*, declares, "Your problem is not your problem; it's the way you handle your problem that is your problem." The problem was not the report. The problem was not the land. Everything God had promised was there. The problem was fear.

> *There is no shame in admitting that we need God's help. He is the Deliverer.*

There will come a time in each of our lives when we have to walk by faith. We see the possibilities, but the problems seem *larger than we are.* Problems of this magnitude require trusting a higher power. Give them to God. There is no shame in admitting that we need God's help. He is the Deliverer.

OBSTACLES OR OPPORTUNITIES

The Chinese language is composed of characters that form words. The Chinese word for *crisis* is made up of two characters: *wei*, meaning "danger," and *ji*, meaning "opportunity." Thus, the Chinese view a crisis not as two separate realities, but as two sides of the same reality containing both danger and opportunity. It becomes a tragedy only if we fail to see the opportunity. Consider the following biblical examples:

- Joseph went through the dungeon to get to the king's palace.

- David went through the battlefield to get to the throne.

- Joshua went through the wilderness to get to Canaan.

Promotion often comes through problem situations. Every solution that exists came to us because of a problem. Some hold the mistaken concept that Christians should not have problems. Nevertheless, we face all of the same circumstances in our lives that non-Christians do. The difference is in how we handle them. If we choose to handle them the same way as the non-Christians, we will get identical results. If we allow God to direct us in handling our problems, He can turn even a tragedy into a triumph.

REJECTING GOD

The Israelites reacted in such a way that God had to step in. Their fury rose to the point that they wanted to get rid of Moses, stone Joshua and Caleb, and go back to Egypt. As they were getting ready to collect the stones, the Shekinah cloud came out of the tabernacle, and God spoke to Moses,

How long shall I bear with this evil congregation who complain against Me? I have heard the complaints which the children of Israel make against Me. Say to them, "As I live," says the LORD, "just as you have spoken in My hearing, so I will do to you: the carcasses of you who have complained against Me shall fall in this wilderness, all of you who were numbered, according to your entire number, from twenty years old and above. Except for Caleb the son of Jephunneh and Joshua the son of Nun, you shall by no means enter the land which I swore I would make you dwell in. But your little ones, whom you said would be victims, I will bring in, and they shall know the land which you have despised....According to the number of the days in which you spied out the land, forty days, for each day you shall bear your guilt one year, namely forty years, and you shall know My rejection. I the LORD have spoken this; I will surely do so to all this evil congregation who are gathered together against Me. In this wilderness they shall be consumed, and there they shall die.'" (Numbers 14:27–31, 34–35)

The people trembled as Moses relayed God's pronounced judgment on them: one year in the wilderness for every day the spies searched out the land. The spies were gone forty days, so a sentence of forty years was handed down. The people left the camp of Kadesh in defeat. God declared that everyone over the age of twenty years would die in the next forty years, with the exceptions of Joshua and Caleb.

What a tragedy! Approximately 1.2 million men and women would die during this period of time. Individual burials would have required eighty-five funerals daily. If there were twelve hours of daylight, they would have conducted seven funerals every hour of the day.

A quote by Henry Ford may apply here: "Whether you think you can or think you can't—you are right."

GETTING RID OF FEAR

PERSONAL EVALUATION

Read each of the following statements and answer **True** or **False**.

1. I sometimes feel like giving up when I'm stressed.

2. Sometimes my fear hinders my faith.

3. Fear has changed the way I see myself.

4. I am a courageous person.

5. Fear has robbed me of good opportunities.

6. I realize there is opportunity in every obstacle.

7. I truly believe God wants me to live in victory.

PERSONAL REFLECTION

Meditate on the following questions and answer them honestly.

1. At the level of faith at which I am operating now, which group of spies would I most likely have sided with—the ten spies who gave the bad report, or the two who gave the good report?

2. Do I overreact to situations and create problems for myself?

3. Do I see myself as a spiritual giant or a spiritual grasshopper?

4. Am I easily intimidated? (If the answer to this is yes, please read Ezekiel 2.)

GROUP DISCUSSION

1. Discuss the following two statements:

   • Faith is the force that activates God's power in our lives.

   • Fear is the force that activates Satan's power in our lives.

2. Discuss the subject of courage, using the following statements as guidelines:

   • Fear refines courage.

   • Courage takes you across the finish line.

   • Courage is doing what you're afraid to do.

   • There can be no courage unless you're scared.

3. Discuss the following statement on character: "Your character is what you really are, while your reputation is merely what others think you are."

4. Discuss God's promise to give the Israelites a land flowing with milk and honey, and decide whether the group feels that God kept His part of the promise.

5. Have a member of the group share a personal experience when a crisis offered two roads—one that led to opportunity, and the other that led to tragedy.

GROUP EXERCISE

The project assignment is to collect "good reports" for an entire week. It will take some effort, but the results will be both positive and rewarding. Group members should simply interview people who have "good news" to share. They can write out the reports or have others write or type them out for them. In the next group meeting, read the good reports that have been collected. This exercise is a faith builder.

chapter 10

GETTING RID OF MEDIOCRITY

FORTY YEARS OF WANDERING

The carcasses of you who have complained against Me shall fall in this wilderness, all of you who were numbered, according to your entire number, from twenty years old and above. Except for Caleb the son of Jephunneh and Joshua the son of Nun.... And your sons shall be shepherds in the wilderness forty years, and bear the brunt of your infidelity, until your carcasses are consumed in the wilderness. According to the number of the days in which you spied out the land, forty days, for each day you shall bear your guilt one year, namely forty years, and you shall know My rejection.   (Numbers 14:29–30, 33–34)

Some people want to get somewhere, but they haven't made up their minds where they are going, so they remain stuck in the same place. Others want to get somewhere, so they move forward, but they have no idea where they are headed. Then there are those who want to get somewhere, know where they are headed, and believe that with determination and direction they will arrive at their destination.

The Israelites set out on a journey to leave Egypt and go into Canaan. God's plan would have allowed them to become victorious in the land of Canaan. However, they became their own hindrances.

Getting out of Egypt is one thing, but getting Egypt out of us takes commitment. Only after doing that can we be conquerors.

THE LAND OF WANDERING

God did not intend for the children of Israel to wander for forty years. Egypt to Canaan was only an eighteen-day journey, which He intended to be stretched into eighteen months of pre-victory training. When the Israelites succumbed to fear, they forfeited the victory and had to roam the wilderness. *This is the land of mediocrity.* People who refuse to learn have to go through the same problems over and over. Life becomes an endless cycle of the same old thoughts, the same old scenes, and the same old surroundings. It is like an electric train under the Christmas tree that keeps circling. You never have to wonder if it's going to make a turn, make a stop to pick up a new passenger, or even slow down. At first, the train is intriguing. But after a while, it becomes monotonous.

> *Mediocrity paints life with a tinge of hopelessness—not enough to keep you discouraged, but just enough to keep you from dreaming.*

You certainly don't have to look far to see mediocrity. In many cases, it's like a curse handed down from generation to generation. It simply means "to settle for less." Mediocrity means living life in a state of complacency bordered on every side by perceived limitations, financial impediments, and rude awakenings. There are no plans for escape.

- Mediocrity is the high school graduate who is content to work the rest of his or her life on a low-income scale—with no plans for the future.

- Mediocrity woos the young couple who heads into life satisfied just to keep up with the Joneses, never stopping to think about their true potential—content to remain as they are.

- Mediocrity serenades the middle-aged person who, at the age of forty-five, feels as if life has been lived to its fullest—who settles in and avoids further challenges.

- Mediocrity paints life with a tinge of hopelessness—not enough to keep you discouraged, but just enough to keep you from dreaming.

The struggle in the land of mediocrity is always there. It is a life of limitations—limited finances, limited adventures, and limited achievements.

George and Candy (again, not their real names) were both born with talents in music, arts, and crafts—gifts that would impress any talent scout. Both chose not to go to college. They could have afforded it, but college would have delayed their plans. As many young couples do, they made choices based on the present, giving little or no thought to the future. Yes, they knew the future would eventually come around, but their attitude was, "We'll just cross that bridge when we get to it." They just had to have what they wanted—immediately.

The first road sign pointing to the land of mediocrity says, *Now*. This is good advice for a procrastinator, but it is not the best recommendation for the planner. George and Candy got married *now*, they had children *now*, and they bought "things" *now*. The years rolled by and they were still living in a rented home, driving old cars, and working for low wages. Because of their "now" philosophy, they *now* work longer hours than others because they make so little. Needless to say, they both work two jobs, which, when combined, do not match the income of one individual with a bachelor's degree. *Now*, both are at the age of fifty, but life looks the same as it did when they were the age of twenty and thirty.

Life in the land of mediocrity seems to go in circles. I wonder what George and Candy will do when they turn seventy and can no longer work long hours. They will have no home, no retirement funds, no investments, and no plan.

> *The choice is yours: Settle for the land of mediocrity or fight for the land of milk and honey.*

I hope they are able to cross that bridge when they get to it. *Now*, their children are married and are making similar choices. Both George and Candy possessed immense talent and charm, but they settled for mediocrity.

"Are they happy?" you might ask. That is the goal, isn't it? If happiness is just acceptance of what life gives you, then perhaps they are. However, if happiness is fulfilling your potential, living your life to its fullest, and making a difference in the lives of others...well, they have never experienced those things to their full measure.

Mediocrity has been called by many names. Max Lucado calls it "the thief of familiarity" (*He Still Moves Stones*). John Mason describes it as "the enemy called average" (*An Enemy Called Average*). Pastor Rick Renner calls it "the land of dream thieves" (*Dream Thieves*). It is a place of bondage, a field of futility, the land of the lost. One thing is certain: those who dwell in the land of wandering never have settled hearts. Such people have no direction, no and no joy. They never taste the meal of a champion. Durin, Israelites' many years of wandering, they made many stops. These were significant mainly because of the need to bury their dead.

THE LAND OF WINNING

God made you a winner. You may be at the same crossroads that Israel faced. Your choice is this: Settle for the land of mediocrity or fight for the land of milk and honey. God prepared you to be a winner, but you must keep your sights on Canaan. The excess baggage that keeps you from running the race with swiftness must be left behind.

Four things will determine whether or not you will reach your God-given potential.

1. You Must Trust God and Take a Risk

You have to take a risk to win. Do something bigger than yourself! That's where God is. The world is filled with overcomers—men and women who stood against the odds and won.

In the early history of the twentieth century, a man decided to start a new business. He wanted to make cars. The public rejected the idea, making a joke of his "smoking machine." His first attempt failed in the first year. He tried again and ended up bankrupt. Determined to win, he tried the same business the third time. This time he did well. That man was Henry Ford.

Another company that took the risk was the Coca-Cola Company, which sold only four hundred Cokes the first year. Today they have a worldwide presence.

Another man wrote children's books. The first twenty-three publishers to which he submitted his stories rejected him. The twenty-fourth publisher took the risk, and the first edition sold six million copies. That man was Theodore Seuss Geisel—better known as Dr. Seuss.

2. You Must Be Willing to Sacrifice

Few people sacrifice anything just for today. You sacrifice only because you see the big picture. You give up something small today for something gigantic tomorrow. John Maxwell is quoted as having said, "There is no success without sacrifice. If I succeed without sacrifice, it's because someone went before me and sacrificed."

Pastor Tommy Barnett left his church in Iowa to become the pastor of Phoenix First Assembly. The church he was pastoring averaged five thousand people. The Phoenix congregation was under a thousand. Through commitment and sacrifice, he now pastors the second-largest church in the nation with a membership of over seventeen thousand.

At the age of forty, Harland Sanders started cooking and selling chicken for customers of his gas station. Since there was no restaurant, customers ate the chicken in his living quarters. Today, Colonel Sanders' Kentucky Fried Chicken franchise serves millions worldwide.

3. You Must Be Willing to Help Other People

Zig Ziglar says, "The best way to ensure to get what you want out of life is to help enough other people get what they want." We must accept the fact that we cannot make it without other people. Every talent God gives us links us to a harvest of people. Each harvest is unique. The unique combination of gifts and talents that an individual possesses will open up a field of people that no one else has been designed to reach.

Many have the mistaken idea that stardom is all about promoting oneself. Exposure certainly is necessary to attain celebrity status, but what really makes a star is giving the public the product or service it demands.

Living life from a selfish perspective limits our effectiveness to others. It is only when people perceive that you are interested in helping them that you will be in demand. Give people what they want, and they will come back for more. If you take only what you want, they may never return. The idea here is not to achieve stardom but rather to make a difference in the lives of others. You may become a star and not even know it.

4. You Must Begin to Make Long-range Choices

You can choose to live for the present, or you can make choices that will affect you throughout eternity. In his book *Seven Habits of Highly Effective People*, Stephen Covey writes, "Begin with the end in mind." This concept does not suggest that we simply look at the bottom line or finished product, but rather at how it will affect our lives in the end.

One of the exercises I use in counseling is to have an individual write his or her own eulogy. The discoveries are amazing. The idea is to write things you would like people to say at your funeral. I have yet to have one of my clients tell me that this is a difficult assignment. We must get out of the habit of thinking only of the present, and train ourselves to think long-range—all the way to the end, if necessary.

> *The unique combination of gifts and talents that an individual possesses will open up a harvest field of people that no one else has been designed to reach.*

While I was attending a seminar several years ago, the instructor asked us to write down twenty-five things we wanted to do before we died. After we had finished this assignment, he stated that we had just joined the ranks of only 3 percent of people who had ever completed such a task.

One afternoon my phone rang. On the other end was a distraught pastor who told me how he and his wife had lost interest in the ministry. He continued by saying that she had isolated herself from him and the church and was displaying anger in her attitudes and conversations.

After listening to him for a few minutes, I asked him when he had noticed a difference in her behavior. He told me that it started in January when he published his goals for the church that year. Upon his showing them to her, she replied, "Now where are the goals for our family this year?"

He remembered her comment only after I probed his memory. It was obvious that he had focused so much on the church that he had completely omitted planning for his family. Afterward he regrouped and devised a plan for his life that included the following order of priorities:

1. God
2. Family
3. Self
4. Friends
5. Church
6. Lifetime achievements

CANAAN IS STILL WAITING TO BE CONQUERED

Joshua and Caleb never stopped believing God's promises. Even though they were opposed by the multitude, they kept their eyes on Canaan. They could not get the taste of Canaan's luscious grapes out of their mouths. Their determination was greater than the challenges facing them. Their thoughts of Canaan grew in magnitude during the forty years of wandering. You see, they had stepped into the Land of Promise. It took only one look to convince them that it would be worth the fight.

A LESSON IN REPELLING

A few years ago I spoke to a group at a conference in West Virginia. Part of our group decided to go repelling. Our guide was a fine Christian man who was an experienced rock climber. We found a challenging 150-foot rock ledge that went straight down and over the mouth of a cave. The last twenty-five feet would be a free-hanging experience. I have never been fond of heights, but neither have I shirked a challenge. So I was game.

Joshua and Caleb had stepped into the Land of Promise. It took only one look to convince them that it would be worth the fight.

I watched anxiously as each person took his or her turn. Some quickly slid straight down the rope like repelling out of a helicopter. Others became afraid halfway down and chose to inch their way down. Finally, my turn came. I leaned over the side of the mountain and peered into the gorge. It appeared to be a thousand feet away. I could feel the rush of anxiety. But I had to overcome my fears with courage. There was no way I would back out now. I had climbed the mountain and put on the gear. I was ready. The instructor began to brief me on the things I should expect.

"The only way off the first lip is to lean into the rope in a squatting position and slowly back off the edge of the rocky cliff," he said.

Noticing my apprehension, he drew a spiritual analogy to the experience. I will never forget his instructions:

> There is a man holding onto one rope at the top and another one holding on at the bottom. These are your safety men. If you fall, they will hold you up and gently lower you off the mountain. These represent your prayer partners in life who hold you up during a crisis.
>
> The secret to getting off the mountain is to keep your feet on the rock at all times. Never take your feet off the rock. That rock beneath your feet represents Jesus. You must be able to feel it beneath you at all times. Even though you can't look down and see your next step, as long as you can feel the rock, you know that you are still on the right course.
>
> I will be the voice that talks you off the mountain. You must not look down or worry about where to step next because I will guide you with my voice. Whatever you do, don't take your eyes off me. If you look down, you might get scared; if you look to the side, you might get confused; if you look straight ahead, you will see only two feet in front of you. Just keep your eyes on me. I represent God the Father in your life. The voice (His Word) will give the direction you need to complete this challenge.
>
> Now you must lean into the rope. The rope is the only tangible guide you have. It never leaves your side. You may cling to it, or even hug it, but never let it go. The rope you are leaning on is already at the bottom waiting for you. That rope represents the Holy Spirit

in your life. Each time you take a step while clinging
or leaning to it, remember, it's already there waiting.
Just trust it.

I didn't quit. I steadily walked off the side of that 150-foot rock ledge. I did step into a couple of potholes, but my safety men, my guide, my rock, and my rope got me safely through.

Never give up!

GETTING RID OF MEDIOCRITY

PERSONAL EVALUATION

Read each of the following statements and answer **True** or **False**.

1. I am determined to be a winner.

2. I am willing first to conquer myself in order to conquer life.

3. I have been wandering in the land of mediocrity longer than I should.

4. I have been willing to settle for less in certain areas of my life instead of trusting God to give me what He promised belongs to me as His child.

5. I haven't been patiently waiting for God's promises but rather taking what I could get in order to have it *now*.

6. I have been afraid to take a risk.

7. I have a distinct plan for my life.

8. I am willing to make sacrifices today in order to be a winner tomorrow.

PERSONAL REFLECTION

Meditate on the following questions and answer them honestly.

1. Do I really know what I want in life?

2. Do I know God's will for my life?

3. Do I have long-range plans and short-term goals to help me accomplish these plans?

4. Am I willing to commit to never giving up no matter what?

GROUP DISCUSSION

1. Discuss the importance of having a plan for your life.

2. Discuss the idea of "settling for less" in order to have what you want now.

3. Discuss the following statements about living in the "land of winning":

   • You must trust God and take a risk.

   • You must be willing to sacrifice.

   • You must be willing to help other people.

   • You must begin to make long-range choices.

4. Ask a member of the group to share a personal experience or the experience of another in which he or she was settling for mediocrity until God convinced him or her that being a winner was possible.

5. Discuss what it is like to live in spiritual Canaan.

6. Discuss the illustration about repelling and how it relates to our own experiences in life.

GROUP EXERCISE

Ask each person to sit in a chair facing the wall. (This will help each person to focus on the exercise.) Give each of them a writing tablet and a pencil. The following exercise will help the members of the group to begin making long-range plans for their lives. First, ask them to write down twenty things they would like to do before they die. Next, they should write down five things they would like to accomplish this year. Last, ask them to write ten statements they would like to have said about them at their funerals. This exercise may take a little time, but it will be very rewarding to the members of the group in determining direction for their lives.

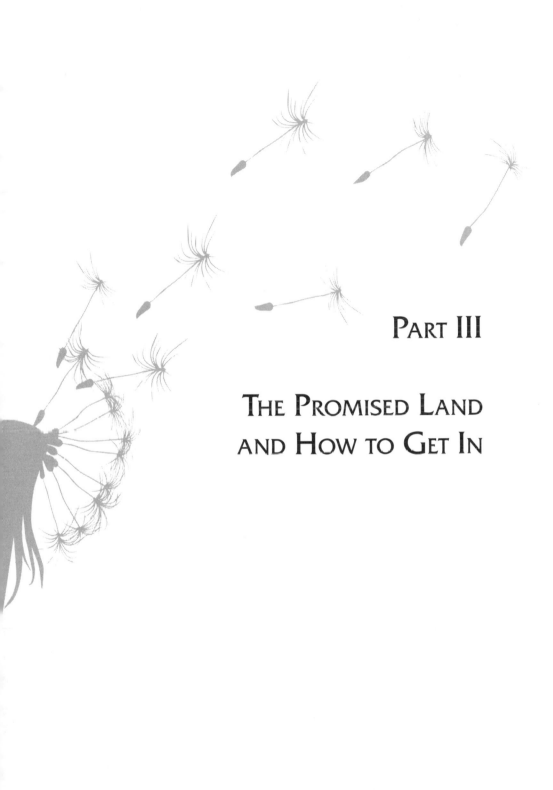

PART III

THE PROMISED LAND AND HOW TO GET IN

At the Door of Your Promise

The generation before had grown accustomed to the miracles of God so much that they became a part of everyday living. Manna here, quail there, a pillar of fire here, and a cloud over there. Yet, even the parting of the great Red Sea and the destruction of their foes did not strengthen their faith enough to believe God for the Promised Land. This new generation grew up knowing only death, funerals, and wandering in the wilderness. They had heard about the miracles, but now they desperately needed to see God's hand working in their own generation.

They were leaving their past behind them and moving into the promises forfeited by their forefathers. They should have been born on this land; they should have been raised on this land; they should already have been worshipping on this land. Even though they had been delayed, their promise had not been denied!

Their desire for the Promised Land created a hunger for God and His presence. Victory is preceded by a season of hunger and thirst. The young, inexperienced priests of Israel lined up to bear the ark of the covenant and go ahead of the people into the land. Little did they know they were about to enter into two new covenants with God: one of water and one of blood.

chapter 11

THE STEP BEFORE
THE FINAL STEP

CROSSING THE JORDAN
AND CAMPING AT GILGAL

*Now the people came up from the Jordan on the tenth day of the
first month, and they camped in Gilgal on the east border of Jericho. And those twelve stones which they took out of the Jordan,
Joshua set up in Gilgal. Then he spoke to the children of Israel,
saying: "When your children ask their fathers in time to come,
saying, 'What are these stones?' then you shall let your children
know, saying, 'Israel crossed over this Jordan on dry land'; for
the* LORD *your God dried up the waters of the Jordan before you
until you had crossed over, as the* LORD *your God did to the Red
Sea, which He dried up before us until we had crossed over....
At that time the* LORD *said to Joshua, "Make flint knives for
yourself, and circumcise the sons of Israel again the second time."
So Joshua made flint knives for himself, and circumcised the sons
of Israel at the hill of the foreskins. And this is the reason why
Joshua circumcised them: all the people who came out of Egypt
who were males, all the men of war, had died in the wilderness*

149

on the way, after they had come out of Egypt. For all the people who came out had been circumcised, but all the people born in the wilderness, on the way as they came out of Egypt, had not been circumcised. (Joshua 4:19–23; 5:2–5)

After forty years of wandering, the morning finally came for these pilgrims to take the first step into the Promised Land. Just on the other side of the Jordan River was milk and honey, but first came the river. Joshua was sure that God would part the water for them as He had for Moses and the former generation. In the case of the Red Sea, an east wind had blown all night and parted the water. When the Israelites came to the Jordan, however, the wind was still and calm. Step-by-step, the young Levites moved toward the muddy Jordan. The water streamed by in a steady flow of swirls and undercurrents, but there was still no parting.

Each one looked at the others as if to say, "What now?" With tenacity, the priests walked forward. They had come too far to even think about going back. They took their first step onto the muddy banks of the mighty Jordan. Still there was no move of God. With swelling faith and determination, they pursued their march into the river, bearing the ark on their shoulders. Once they were into the water, they noticed the currents of the river suddenly stopping. The river began to rise up like a wall. And for the first time in centuries, the secrets that lay underneath Jordan's waters were revealed—smooth stones in the riverbed. The children of Israel walked across on a dry path.

Just after the last tribe had crossed, Joshua instructed the leaders to pick up twelve stones and carry them from the riverbed to the camp, where they set up a memorial. (See Joshua 4:1–9.) Joshua may have addressed the pilgrims of faith by saying something to this effect: "The stones we leave here by the Jordan signify our hard, rough life in the wilderness. The smooth stones we extricated as a memorial signify our lives we will cleanse before God this day. These stones were cleaned and purified by the washing of the water until all the rough edges were removed. So shall we be this day before the Lord of Hosts."

The Bible is explicit in noting that during the crossing of the Jordan, the river *"rose in a heap very far away at Adam, the city that is beside Zaretan"* (Joshua 3:16). Every person all the way back to Adam was represented by the twelve stones Joshua took from the Jordan to build a memorial unto the Lord. One could compare this river crossing to baptism by water and the need to have the physical experience of going into the water as a testimonial of the inward work of grace in the heart.

> *Gilgal represents a place of "rolling away," or getting rid of things that hinder our stewardship when we come into the place of God's favor and blessings.*

GILGAL, THE PLACE OF SANCTIFICATION

"Now the people came up from the Jordan on the tenth day of the first month, and they camped in Gilgal" (Joshua 4:19). Gilgal seems like a strange name for such a serene place. It means "circle of standing stones."

> *Then the LORD said to Joshua, "This day I have rolled away the reproach of Egypt from you." Therefore the name of the place is called Gilgal to this day.* (Joshua 5:9)

God can give us His promises at will, but with each blessing comes the responsibility to share the blessing. God's blessings are not given to be stored up as earthly treasures. Rather, they are given to increase the kingdom of God. Before God can give us His gifts, He takes us through a period of cleansing and purification so we will not be tempted to abuse His gifts.

Gilgal represents a place of "rolling away," or getting rid of things that hinder our stewardship when we come into the place of God's favor and blessings.

THE COVENANT OF BLOOD

Joshua gathered the men of each tribe and assembled them at the tabernacle. Then he began telling the story of Abraham and their forefathers. He reminded them of how God had commanded them to circumcise their race as a covenant of blood with God. The shedding of blood goes all the way back to the garden of Eden after the fall of Adam. (See Genesis 3:21.)

Even though we are not offering literal, physical blood, the fact remains that when we come to God in repentance, He looks to the cross, where Jesus, the spotless Lamb, died and placed our sins under the blood. Jesus' sacrifice paid for our sins. Spiritually speaking, at that moment of redemption, our spirits were transfused and transformed from being dead to having a living, purpose-driven existence. We have now been washed in the blood. That's why Robert Lowry articulated in his nineteenth-century hymn,

> What can wash away my sin?
> Nothing but the blood of Jesus;
> What can make me whole again?
> Nothing but the blood of Jesus.
> O! precious is the flow
> That makes me white as snow;

No other fount I know,

Nothing but the blood of Jesus.

—Robert Lowry, 1876

As Easy as A-B-C

Just as with Joshua's generation, we too must experience a "spiritual circumcision":

> *In Him you were also circumcised with the circumcision made without hands, by putting off the body of the sins of the flesh, by the circumcision of Christ, buried with Him in baptism, in which you also were raised with Him through faith in the working of God, who raised Him from the dead.*
>
> (Colossians 2:11–12)

Since the death and resurrection of Christ, God has made it easy for us to be saved. It's as easy as A–B–C. Here is a simple formula, based on Romans 10:9:

A. Admit that you have sinned.

B. Believe that Christ died for your sins.

C. Confess that He is Lord of your life.

Water and Blood

We have these two witnesses with us: water and blood. They are often found linked together throughout Scripture, and with good reason.

- Water and blood flowed from the body of Jesus as the last physical evidence of His crucifixion. (See John 19:34.)

- Water and blood reminded Pilate that he had killed an innocent man. (See Matthew 27:24.)

- Water and blood were used by the high priest of the Old Testament to offer up sacrifices to God. (See Leviticus 7, 8.)
- Water and blood are parts of the birthing process.

The relationship between these two elements is quite simple. They testify to the triune entity of man, reminding us that we are made in God's image—body, soul, and spirit.

Water and blood are natural elements of the body, yet both play significant roles in helping us to understand God's spiritual plan for man. The blood cleanses our spirits by washing us in the blood of Christ; the water cleanses our souls, which are our minds, by washing us in the water of the Word.

> *Husbands, love your wives, just as Christ also loved the church and gave Himself for her, that He might sanctify and cleanse her with the washing of water by the word, that He might present her to Himself a glorious church, not having spot or wrinkle or any such thing, but that she should be holy and without blemish.* (Ephesians 5:25–27)

WASHING OF THE WORD

Although the washing by the blood is an instantaneous work of God, the washing by the water of the Word is a continual process called *sanctification*. Just as we bathe our bodies each day, so should we bathe our souls daily with the Word of God. A lack of cleansing by the Word is the essential reason many fail to live in victory. They march into battle without having their minds conditioned for war. They declare war on their enemy, but they have a limited knowledge as to how to survive the war, once engaged in battle.

There is no victory without the daily washing by the Word. It not only makes *a* difference, but it is also *the* difference between

154

victorious living and mediocre living. There is no substitute for a good bath. Cologne can't hide filth, fresh clothes can't hide stench, and a hat can't cleanse dirty hair. In the same way, only the Word of God can remove the filth from our minds and the stench from our attitudes. That is why the apostle Paul wrote, *"Be transformed by the renewing of your mind"* (Romans 12:2) through the Word of God. That is also why he said that *"faith comes by hearing, and hearing by the word of God"* (Romans 10:17).

The step before the final step of entering into the land of promise is a time of cleansing through repentance—putting our sins under the blood and receiving more of God's thoughts than this world's thoughts. Once we apply His Word to our lives, He reveals areas of impurity that need to be cleansed by His blood. Each day God orders our steps with His Word as we are transformed more and more into His likeness.

> *Only the Word of God can remove the filth from our minds and the stench from our attitudes.*

SANCTIFICATION:
THE STEP BEFORE THE FINAL STEP

PERSONAL EVALUATION & REFLECTION

Meditate on the following questions and answer them honestly.

1. Can you honestly say that you are hungry and thirsty for God? *(Before answering this question, think back to the last time you were truly hungry or thirsty and remember your search to find food or drink.)*

2. Do you feel like the former Israelite generation who took God's blessings for granted?

3. Do you ever find yourself basing your faith only on the stories of another generation, or are you also telling your own stories about your journey with God?

4. Have you ever found yourself turning back just before the victory? Remember the faith of those young Levites who stepped into the Jordan River before the waters parted.

5. How much do you actually read the Bible?

6. How many Scriptures could you quote if you did not have your Bible near you? Do you have a favorite Scripture?

7. Do you know how to lead someone to Christ? Have you ever done it? When was the last time?

Group Discussion

1. Discuss the twelve stones that were taken out of the riverbed. Discuss the significance of the memorial built in Gilgal.

2. Ask a member of the group to relate a story that was handed down from a grandparent or older Christian person that has strengthened his or her faith.

3. Discuss the importance of the cleansing process before the victory.

4. Explain what is meant by the following statement: "Gilgal represents a place of 'rolling away,' or getting rid of things that hinder our stewardship when we come into the place of God's favor and blessings."

5. Discuss the roles of the water and the blood in helping us to understand God's spiritual plan for man.

6. How does the washing of the Word make the difference between victorious living and mediocre living?

7. Discuss the importance of naming a memorial.

8. Repeat the A–B–C plan of salvation until the entire group knows it by heart. Help the group memorize Romans 10:9 while in class by repeating it several times.

9. Ask if someone in the group can describe how the washing of the Word *purges* an individual.

10. Discuss the last sentence in this chapter: "Each day God orders our steps with His Word."

GROUP EXERCISE

Build yourself a memorial. It may only be a small one of stones or perhaps of wood. Build it with your own hands and give it a name. The Bible is filled with named altars. Each name signifies of a time when God met with His people and brought deliverance. Don't tear it down. It will be a landmark of faith for the rest of your journey with God.

chapter 12

At Last—Due Season

Possessing Your Promises

And let us not grow weary while doing good, for in due season we shall reap if we do not lose heart. (Galatians 6:9)

As a baby is delivered after hours of labor and months of anticipation, all the pain is forgotten. At last, you have a tiny human form to hold—hands to clasp, lips to kiss, and baby's breath on your cheek. The struggling is over and the final days of discomfort diminish in the face of the miracle you hold in your arms. The only thought you can conceive in this breathtaking moment of awe is that it was worth it all.

Similarly, possessing your promise makes life worth the steep climb. Holding on to the reality that was once only a dream brings such contentment that you drop to your knees, lift your hands, and worship the One who never fails to fulfill His promises to every pilgrim.

Canaan Land

The red-faced, battle-scarred caravan finally arrived in the Land of Promise. It was everything they had imagined it would be—and

159

more. With the desert behind them, they began to look ahead. First, God gave them Jericho, but it was only the first of many cities and many battles. Each day, the caravan pushed forward, conquering new territory and leaving a remnant of relatives behind. The tribe of Simeon was first to settle. They immediately began building walls and altars to secure their land. Next, the tribe of Judah settled just south of Jericho. The Israelite army downsized each time a city was captured because more tribes became settlers—at home in their promised land.

Eastward and northward they pushed, claiming everything in their path. The rich, fertile land had already been worked. God sometimes allows our enemies to work the land while He is storing it up for His children. The desert lessons were behind them and a new breed of God-fearing pilgrims emerged. The colors of Israel began to fly in every city; soon the land would be theirs.

> *God did not call you to be hungry, lonely, isolated, and depressed. He created you to show forth His glory, to demonstrate His power, and to fulfill His will!*

"Ah, Canaan land, and what's even better, it is *our* land," cried the fathers of Israel. The richness of the soil extended the growing season to produce twice the number of crops they had had in Egypt. There were fruit trees by the scores and an abundance of cool, fresh water. The wells ran deep, the breeze remained steady, and the favor of God stilled the fear of enemy uprisings. Home at last; peace at last; joy at last! It was worth the journey.

Imagine that first evening in Canaan—a night of celebration. Tambourines, timbrels, and psalteries accompanied the dancing. The joyful praise electrified the air. The old men cried and the young men laughed, while the women talked of children growing up in new houses. Food was plentiful! Manna and quail were out; spicy herbs and fresh vegetables were in. The menu for that first feast likely included cooked meat and vegetables sautéed in garlic and onions, with honey, melons, and berries for dessert. It was truly the land of milk and honey. Their promise had been fulfilled. They were destined to win.

SATAN FEARS YOUR COMING INTO YOUR PROPHETIC SEASON

The enemy is terrified of people who have been sanctified. He sets traps to steal their joy and hinder them from coming into their prophetic season. Satan tries to rip away God's promises until all that is left is a spiritual ghost town, a vacant house. He delights in seeing God's children only going through the motions.

Satan desires to sabotage your success because you were created to win. The Potter molded you in His image. He carefully formed you with His anvil and hammer so you would be strong enough to win. You were designed to be a vessel of honor for the Master's use.

You were created to walk in blessings and not curses. You were created to walk in dignity, not in shame. You were created to hold your head high, to keep going and not quit. You were crafted to soar with the eagles, not to scratch in the dirt with the chickens. You were created to *run and not be weary,...walk and not faint* (Isaiah 40:31). You were not created to be stressed out but to be strong in battle. You were *fearfully and wonderfully made* (Psalm 139:14) in the express image of the God of this universe. You have His seed planted in you. God did not call you to be hungry, lonely, isolated, and depressed. He created you to show forth His glory, to demonstrate His power, and to fulfill His will!

A PROMISE FOR EVERY SEASON OF LIFE

"To everything there is a season, a time for every purpose under heaven" (Ecclesiastes 3:1). Each season comes with fresh perspectives that guide us into the next season of our lives. It is our responsibility to discern the season God has us in. These seasons eventually bring us into the season of promise—our due season.

Due season is the season God promised for the pilgrims who do not grow weary of doing the right things in the midst of adversity. However, when one area is being challenged, God can bring harvest in another area. Our temptation is to focus only on the storm, robbing us of the blessings that are coming into other areas of our lives. Therefore, we need to discern our seasons and understand the purpose of each season in life.

God changes the seasons of life for the same reason He changes the seasons of the earth. This allows us to replenish our losses and rediscover dormant potentials. Every now and then, God airbrushes the earth with a blanket of snow to remind us that winter is a season of beauty as well as recuperation. Winter presents opportunities unknown in the other seasons of life. It is a time for fresh ideas. It is a time to slow down, to pause and think and thank God for what He has kept us from.

Spring is the time to plant. Summer is the season of toil and labor—hard work without seeing the results. Fall is the season for getting ready. Some would say it is the season of harvest, but actually the harvest is a yearlong process. There is a harvest in every season of life.

DUE SEASON

In Galatians 6:9 we read, *"And let us not grow weary while doing good, for in due season we shall reap if we do not lose heart."* If we endure, we will reap in *"due season"*—the season of promise, blessing, and fulfillment. Satan will do everything he can to keep you from due season. He will lure you to take shortcuts because he knows that, in due season, whatever you put your hands to will prosper. Some people never make it to due season because they didn't come through winter, spring, summer, and fall. But for those who go all the way, we have this promise: do not grow weary; *in due season*, you will reap if you do not lose heart!

Business invoices have a space for a due date—a date when payment is due. If you are the payer, it is the day you pay up. If you are the note holder, it is the day when you are paid. There is another statement that says, "Penalty for late payment."

God allows us to go through seasons that strengthen our faith. He not only ordained a beginning for that season, but He also ordained an end. He is not only the Alpha, but He is

> *God is not only the Alpha, but He is also the Omega. God has ordained a day when your season of struggle is over.*

also the Omega. God has ordained a day when the season of struggle is over. It is a divine eviction notice for the devil, which says, "Your time is up!"

Then, I can say, "Devil, today my due season starts. I worked for it. I paid for it. I walked by faith for it. I pressed on when I wanted to quit. I prayed when I wanted to sleep. I fasted when I wanted to eat. I worked when I wanted to play. But today is payday! Today your hold is broken, your tricks are all played out, and your accusations are no longer valid. The Court has just handed down the final judgment in my favor, and the Judge says you have to pay up. Pack up and get out of town. God has invoked a restraining order against you during my *due season*! It's my time, my harvest, and my season of blessing!"

LIVING IN CANAAN

I once was a slave living in Egypt, but now I'm free and living in Canaan. Canaan land is not heaven—it is a life of victory here on earth. Once in Canaan, the desire to return to Egypt is gone. The bitterness of life was sweetened at the camp in Marah. The habit of murmuring and complaining was broken at Rephidim by divine intervention. The mountaintop experience of Sinai took care of all doubt. Stress was released at Taberah, and fear was banished at Kadesh Barnea. No more living in mediocrity; the wandering years are behind. Now we can say with Caleb, "Give me this mountain. This pilgrim is receiving the promise!" (See Joshua 14:6–13.)

At Last—Due Season

Personal Evaluation

Look up Scriptures that you can claim to bring you into *due season*. Write them down and memorize them. The following guide will help you determine areas of your life where you need to claim His promises.

1. What is your promise for health?

2. What is your promise for success?

3. What is your promise for your finances?

4. What is your promise for your marriage?

5. What is your promise for your children?

6. What is your promise for heaven?

7. What is your promise for hope?

8. What is the promise that builds your faith?

9. What is the promise that helps you feel good about yourself?

10. What is the promise that gives you peace about your salvation?

Personal Reflection

Meditate on the following questions and answer them honestly.

1. Do I really believe God is who He says He is?

2. Do I really believe God can do what He says He can do?

3. Do I really believe I am who God says I am?

4. Do I really believe I can do what God says I can do?

5. Do I know the assignment God has given to me for my life?

Group Discussion

1. Discuss ways Satan tries to keep you from your due season.

2. Discuss ways of knowing that you are coming into due season.

3. Discuss how many due seasons a person may have in his or her lifetime.

4. Discuss whether or not a person can have due season in one area and a season of labor in another area.

5. Discuss why we need a getting-ready season to precede due season.

6. Discuss this Scripture: *"Let us not grow weary while doing good"* (Galatians 6:9).

7. Discuss this statement: "Satan does not want you to come into your season of fulfillment."

8. Discuss seasons in life for which you couldn't initially understand the purpose but realized later that God used those hard seasons to do a good work in you.

GROUP EXERCISE

Have each member of the group write one statement that sums up the assignment God has given to him or her in this life. Then have each member read the statement before the group.

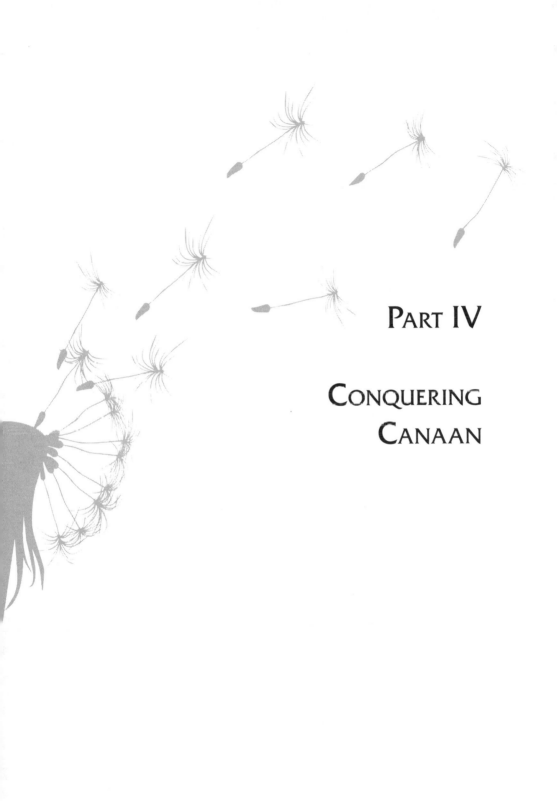

PART IV

CONQUERING
CANAAN

THE LAND OF CANAAN

Canaan land. Where is it? Is it heaven, or is it here on earth? All my life I've heard songs about Canaan land. One song said it was just in sight, yet another told me it was just across the chilly Jordan. My favorite description was the one that said,

> *Egypt was once my home, I was a slave.*
> *Helpless in sin did roam, love light did crave,*
> *But when I looked up to heaven's dome,*
> *Christ came to save, I'm livin' in Canaan now.*

Canaan—the land that flows with milk and honey—was not a promise to those who died. It is a promised for those who dare to really live. It is not just a geographical landmark for ancient Israel; it is a symbol of victorious living!

- Become the landlord of your life.
- Live in blessings.
- Experience a life of courage and triumph.

However, Canaan land does not come prepackaged and wrapped in a bow. The journey through the wilderness toward the promise served as a training ground to fortify the warriors' faith for the rest of the trip. Once in Canaan, it's time to conquer.

Every season has a beginning and an end. There comes a time in each of our lives when we must decide to conquer our Canaan. Through the seasons of struggle, we must resist the subtle temptations of mediocrity and begin to conquer.

Are you ready to change your spiritual address? Canaan is:

- a place of music and laughter

- a place of dancing and glee

- a place of having your enemies under your feet and your hands on the plow

The journey of life has prepared you for this moment, but you must decide. If you do not want to conquer, perhaps you should stop reading here, because the adventure before you requires a will to win, a champion mentality, and, most of all, the vision to see what God knows already exists. That's right—Canaan land!

chapter 13

CONQUERING CANAAN

PREPARING FOR BATTLE

[The LORD said to Joshua] *"Have I not commanded you? Be strong and of good courage; do not be afraid, nor be dismayed, for the LORD your God is with you wherever you go." Then Joshua commanded the officers of the people, saying, "Pass through the camp and command the people, saying, 'Prepare provisions for yourselves, for within three days you will cross over this Jordan, to go in to possess the land which the LORD your God is giving you to possess'."...And Joshua said to the people, "Sanctify your-selves, for tomorrow the LORD will do wonders among you."*

(Joshua 1:9–11; 3:5)

I t's confession time. It was the third night of his first revival. Red-faced with embarrassment, this young minister had a lump in his throat, and his knees were knocking. This was only his seventh sermon. The other six times he preached one of only two sermons he knew. But here he was on the third night of a revival. What would he do? He had already preached all his material.

He was certain that God would come through before it was time to deliver the sermon. He walked to the pulpit with a blank mind and an open Bible. Soon after reading a Scripture he really didn't understand, he asked the pastor of the church to pray. A few words into the pastor's prayer, the young preacher had his first experience with pulpit panic.

He had heard people say, "Just open your mouth and God will fill it." His mouth was open, but the only thing he could think of was finding the closest exit. While the pastor prayed, he closed his brand-new Bible, walked out the side door of the old country church, got in his car, and drove away. Later, he didn't even ask how the pastor had handled the situation when he realized his teenage evangelist had bailed out on him. Somehow he knew the seasoned pastor would understand.

Perhaps you have already figured out from the intimate details that I was that young, green minister. It was my first lesson on preparation. I am not speaking of intellectual preparation, but of spiritual preparation.

GOD'S DRESSING ROOM

As we have seen, before God could take the children of Israel into Canaan, they had to go to Gilgal. This was Israel's last campsite before possessing the Promised Land. It was necessary to prepare them for the challenges they were about to face.

They sat by glimmering campfires as they listened to their new leader. Moses was dead, and Joshua was in charge. Joshua sent the captains of Israel through the campsite with a message: *"Sanctify yourselves, for tomorrow the LORD will do wonders among you"* (Joshua 3:5). Each man, woman, and child knew the routine. They had heard this before and had seen the end result of those who took it lightly. Knowing there could be no victory without sanctification, they began by washing their clothes and their bodies. Each man then searched his tent for any unclean thing that would offend the

Almighty. The routine lasted for three days. They waited anxiously to see what God would do next. After forty years of wandering, they were ready to have their own houses, lands, and gardens. The Lord had promised these things, but first they had to obey His instructions.

THE PURGING

The purpose of sanctification is to set us apart. Perhaps we are set apart so we won't stumble over our sin when the fighting begins. Many times, the process of sanctification requires us to set aside our personal desires until we find our spiritual direction. Even though the process of sanctification never ends, the initial purging is necessary for those who are serious about winning the battle.

God chose Gilgal for their initial purging. As we learned, *Gilgal* means "circle of stones." This was where Israel erected their memorial remembering how God had delivered them. Now, perhaps the encircled stones also represented a group of leaders encircled for a conference. The counsel of God

> *Even though Jericho would be the first city in the Promised Land to fall to the Israelite army, the battle was actually won at Gilgal.*

is a prerequisite for winning. Engaging in warfare without God's leading is spiritual suicide. Even though Jericho would be the first city in the Promised Land to fall to the Israelite army, the battle was actually won at Gilgal.

In boot camp there can be as many as seventy-five platoons on the field at one time, but you are trained to respond to the voice of only one sergeant. The same thing is true on the spiritual battlefield. If you do not know the voice of your Captain, it may cost you your life. This is the purpose of Gilgal.

GOD'S INSTRUCTIONS

And it came to pass, when Joshua was by Jericho, that he lifted his eyes and looked, and behold, a Man stood opposite him with His sword drawn in His hand. And Joshua went to Him and said to Him, "Are You for us or for our adversaries?" So He said, "No, but as Commander of the army of the LORD I have now come." And Joshua fell on his face to the earth and worshipped, and said to Him, "What does my Lord say to His servant?"
(Joshua 5:13–14)

Never go to battle without a plan! At Gilgal, God gave the Israelites the plan for their first battle. The plan was spiritual; no one really understood it at first. The angel told them to march around the walls a total of thirteen times—one for each of the tribes of Israel and one for God—and the walls would fall down. The instructions were specific:

- March around the walls once each day for six days.
- On the seventh day, march around the walls seven times.
- On the seventh trip on the seventh day, shout and blow the trumpets.

So the people shouted when the priests blew with the trumpets:

And it happened when the people heard the sound of the trumpet, and the people shouted with a great shout, that the wall fell down flat. Then the people went up into the city, every man straight before him, and they took the city.   (Joshua 6:20)

Gilgal in St. Louis

The church I pastor is in the St. Louis, Missouri, area. We held our last service in our old church in January 1997. Most people thought we were foolish, since we had no place to go. Usually I don't recommend this method, but I do recommend following God. We had sold our thirty-two-year-old church in hopes of moving the congregation into a strip mall we planned to renovate. The sale was final and the money was in our hands. We didn't expect the deal with the mall to fall through at the last minute. We were a congregation of several hundred people with no place to call home.

God had promised us Canaan, but we didn't know we would have to follow the cloud first. We secured a school gymnasium to worship in. We stepped out in faith and immediately gained sixty people the first month. That location held us for only three months. Our nomadic congregation had already outgrown the space, so we decided to move to a larger gymnasium about seventeen miles away, not knowing if anyone would follow. The statistics were definitely against us.

At Gilgal, God gave the Israelites the plan for their first battle. The plan was spiritual; no one really understood it at first, but they obeyed.

We did our routine—arrive at 5:30 a.m., set up chairs, haul in the PA system, set up the musical instruments, go home and shower, return for the 9:30 a.m. service. We had no idea we would follow this routine for the next two years.

About nine months into our faith journey, we purchased the St. Louis Soccer House, an indoor soccer facility that housed several sports companies, three bars, and one other business. The owners were in bankruptcy court, and it looked like a win-win situation. We continued our Sunday routine, hoping that we could soon begin renovating our new home. However, we would move eighteen more times before calling any one place home.

We were into the third month of paperwork when we realized this was not going to be an easy deal. One complication after another arose. We were sued twice. The suits eventually ended up in the state court system, and we lost. One of the bars and another business forced us to pay their remaining leases.

I kept thinking, *How can things be so complicated? Surely this is the end of the battle.* Three months became six months. Six months became one year. We still didn't have a building permit to begin construction. Yet, we kept growing. By this time we had shed our church clothes because we had to move into a building without air conditioning to accommodate our growing assembly. So, in jeans and golf shirts and with handheld fans, we marched on to church. No one really seemed to mind.

> *After a while, I realized God was telling me to sanctify the people and the land for the conquest He was about to give us—Canaan!*

After a year of this routine, I began to believe that construction might be delayed even longer. I was getting weary of the early Sunday setup, the lack of normality in our church social life, and the ministries that were dying for lack of schedule, place, and equipment. Many ministries began to suffer, even though the worship services remained strong. I prayed for hours, pleading to God for relief. His words seemed somewhat confusing to me at first. He replied, "Go to Gilgal." After a while, I realized He was telling me to sanctify the people and the land for the conquest He was about to give us—Canaan!

I announced that we would be meeting in our empty soccer building. By this time, the artificial turf had been removed and we were worshipping on a dirt floor. I asked everyone to bring a lawn chair and to dress warmly. The people came out in droves to this gathering of warriors. I gave every elder in the church a cement block. We worshipped for a while in the cold building. The people sat behind the elders of their oversight groups. It looked like the twelve tribes of Israel in a massive circle.

> *The people came out in droves to this gathering of warriors....I believe we witnessed a divine visitation from God.*

After we sang, I read the passage about God sending the children of Israel to Gilgal. Each elder came and laid down his cement block and offered a prayer of dedication. As each elder came up, I stacked the blocks, forming an altar. Then we poured a gallon of olive oil on top of the blocks and began our corporate prayer of sanctification and dedication of the land. During the prayer, it began to rain. It rained so hard on the metal roof of the building that we could no longer hear the music or the praying. Everyone became quiet to wait for the rain to end.

Our teens had just returned from a weekend trip and many had left their suitcases outside the building. One of the teens ran out to secure the luggage and came bursting back through the doors, announcing that it was only raining directly over the top of the building. None of the luggage was wet, and the ground and cars were not wet. I believe we witnessed a divine visitation from God.

179

Within days I received a phone call from a St. Louis businessman. He put me in touch with the county commissioner, who arranged a meeting that very afternoon. I went to the meeting and walked out in two hours with the first of twenty-two building permits needed to complete our project. Renovations were underway!

Twin Rivers Worship Center was dedicated in April 1999. It is appraised at several million dollars. Thank God for Gilgal!

Conquering Canaan

Personal Evaluation & Reflection

Meditate on the following questions and answer them honestly.

1. Can you look back over your life and remember a place God took you that had no other purpose than preparation? When is the last time you visited that place?

2. What is God refining in you right now?

3. Look at your preparation process and see if you can determine where God is taking you.

4. Take at least ten minutes to sit in a quiet place and predict how different your life would have been if not for a season of preparation. *(Don't be surprised if this exercise turns into private worship.)*

Group Discussion

1. Discuss God's process of preparation.

2. Ask a member of the group to share an experience of jumping ahead of the process and not allowing God to fully prepare him or her.

3. Discuss the purpose of sanctification.

4. Ask a member of the group to share how God used an adverse circumstance as a purging process in his or her life.

5. Ask the group to discuss the question, "How long does purging last?"

6. Ask the group to share ways God personally speaks to them to give direction.

7. Discuss how to respond to God's instructions when they don't seem to make sense. Use the example of God's instructions to Joshua to march around the walls, blow trumpets, and shout in order to win a battle.

GROUP EXERCISE

Write God a letter and thank Him for your personal Gilgal.

chapter 14

CONQUERING THE CANAANITES

OVERCOMING THE LOVE OF MONEY

*Joshua said, "By this you shall know that the living God is among you, and that He will without fail drive out from before you **the Canaanites** and the Hittites and the Hivites and the Perizzites and the Girgashites and the Amorites and the Jebusites."*
(Joshua 3:10, emphasis added)

But if you do not drive out the inhabitants of the land from before you, then it shall be that those whom you let remain shall be irritants in your eyes and thorns in your sides, and they shall harass you in the land where you dwell. (Numbers 33:55)

Canaanite comes from the Hebrew word *kena'aniy*, which is derived from two words: *kena*, meaning "humiliated" or "brought low," and *kena'an*, meaning "merchant" and "traffic or trade." Together they mean "to be brought low by traffic or trade." In short, the word denotes one whose demise is brought on by greed.

THE PATH OF GREED

In the 1920s, Arthur Fergusen, a Scotsman, had an amazing ability to sell anything. He once "sold" the London Nelson Column in Trafalgar Square to a tourist for $12,000. He received a $1,000 deposit on the sale of Big Ben for the bargain price of $100,000. Then, for an undisclosed amount, he even sold Buckingham Palace.

Obviously, Fergusen was a con man. Since most of the people he defrauded were Americans, he eventually came to the United States and rented the White House to a cattle rancher for $100,000 a year—cash in advance, of course. He then tried to sell the Statue of Liberty by telling an Australian tourist that the port authori-

> *It's not the last step on the path of greed that kills you; it's the first step—the step called envy.*

ties were going to extend the harbor and were planning to tear down the statue. He asked for $100,000 as a deposit. When his money was delayed, Fergusen became agitated. The Australian became suspicious, and, after an investigation, had Fergusen arrested for fraud. He was given a sentence of only five years, after which he was released to enjoy his swindled wealth.

The path of greed will not let you sleep until dirty money is in your hands. Greed causes you to rob your family, your friends—even God. Solomon, the wisest man who ever lived, said, *"Do not enter the path of the wicked, and do not walk in the way of evil....A sound heart is life to the body, but envy is rottenness to the bones"* (Proverbs 4:14; 14:30). It's not the last step on the path of greed that kills you; it's the first step—the step called *envy*. When you envy the wicked, you step into their path, and the addiction begins.

GREED IS AN ANIMAL

Monkeys are greedy creatures. In his commentary on the book of Philippians, James Montgomery Boice tells how monkeys are captured. First, the hunter glues a bottle-necked vase to a heavy board. He then places several marbles inside the vase. The monkey sees the shiny marbles and puts his hand inside to confiscate a fistful. When he tries to retract his clinched fist, it will not fit through the slim neck of the vase. If only he would release a few of the marbles, he could get his fist out. But he will not. The hunter then throws a net over the monkey and puts him in a cage. Even then, the monkey will not release his newfound treasure. The only way to get the monkey's hand out of the bottle is to break the glass. The monkey got what he wanted—marbles—but he lost what he had—his freedom. This is the snare of greed!

THE TITHE OF EDEN

We have to make a place for God to rule in the midst of our world. When God placed Adam and Eve in the garden, He gave them two trees—the Tree of Life and the Tree of Knowledge of Good and Evil. The Tree of Life was to ensure their everlasting relationship with Him. It had the ability to heal them and give them eternal life. The Tree of Knowledge of Good and Evil was the forbidden tree. This tree was the tithe of Eden—the part that belonged to God. Leave it and you will be blessed. Steal it and you will be cursed. Tithing is about giving, but it is more about *not taking* what belongs to God.

THE TITHE OF CANAAN

But all the silver and gold, and vessels of bronze and iron [in Jericho], *are consecrated to the LORD; they shall come into the treasury of the LORD.*   (Joshua 6:19)

The Promised Land also had a tithe—it was called Jericho. God promised to give Israel the land of Canaan, but the promise came with specific instructions: do not take anything from

Jericho. That was the tithe, the part that belonged to God. The only way we can conquer greed is to place God in the middle of the victory.

Jericho was conquered with walls falling, women screaming, warriors marching, kings fleeing, trumpets blowing, and priests dancing. It was such a miraculous "God thing" that no one dared to take any credit.

Scurrying Hebrews, skipping about in victory, made the spirit of the Canaanite rear his head and snarl. Like the serpent in the garden, he was coiled enticingly around his bag of silver and gold, as if to say to an Israelite named Achan, "Come on, take it. It's free money and no one is looking."

> The only way we can conquer greed is to place God in the middle of the victory.

Achan rewarded himself with this gift for being so brave. The old Canaanite spirit hissed in glee because he knew this was the opportunity to infect the Israelites with poisonous greed. Like a shiny, red apple on a forbidden tree, the bag of gold lay in a secret place. When no one was looking, Achan snatched the bag and stuffed it in his side pouch. There was the seed—the only open door the spirit of greed needed. Envy and greed had entered the heart of Achan. *After all*, he thought, *it's only a robe, five pounds of silver, and one and one-fourth pounds of gold. No one will miss it.*

THE LOVE OF DIRTY MONEY

The tithe belongs to God. By giving it, we create a place for God to bless our finances. Keeping the tithe is stealing from the Almighty.

In Joshua 7, Israel goes to war and loses. In desperation, Joshua seeks the Lord and asks,

> *Alas, Lord GOD, why have You brought this people over the Jordan at all; to deliver us into the hand of the Amorites, to destroy us? Oh, that we had been content, and dwelt on the other side of the Jordan! O Lord, what shall I say when Israel turns its back before its enemies? For the Canaanites and all the inhabitants of the land will hear it, and surround us, and cut off our name from the earth. Then what will You do for Your great name?*
>
> (Joshua 7:7–9)

In essence, he was saying, "What happened out there? Why are we not blessed? Why didn't You fight with us today? Didn't You just give us Jericho?"

God's reply to Joshua was not the one he wanted to hear.

> *Get up! Why do you lie thus on your face? Israel has sinned, and they have also transgressed My covenant which I commanded them. For they have even taken some of the accursed things, and have both stolen and deceived; and they have also put it among their own stuff. Therefore the children of Israel could not stand before their enemies, but turned their backs before their enemies, because they have become doomed to destruction.*
>
> (Joshua 7:10–12)

Joshua commanded the head of every household to come before him and give glory to God. Achan's sin was revealed as he confessed to Joshua. Not only did he steal the garment and the gold and silver, but he also became stale in his worship. Achan and his family died that day along with the curse of the Canaanite. The small bag of silver and gold was returned to Jericho to lie amid the rubble. The next day, Israel won again.

THE LOVE OF BLESSED MONEY

Greed is an expensive vice. The love of dirty money will eventually cost more than it gives. Victorious people love money, too; they just love a different type. They love "blessed money."

First Timothy 6:9–10 says,

> *But those who desire to be rich fall into temptation and a snare, and into many foolish and harmful lusts which drown men in destruction and perdition. For the love of money is a root of all kinds of evil, for which some have strayed from the faith in their greediness, and pierced themselves through with many sorrows.*

The cure for greed is giving. It is simply impossible to give yourself into greed. The love of money is a snare only to those who have the wrong motives.

Many of God's heroes were wealthy men. Some, like Job, were the wealthiest men in the world during their era. You can love money when you're giving it away. Blessed money is any money that has been tithed to God and used as He directs. It is the only real assurance for long-term financial victory.

THE T.Y.E.N. PRINCIPLE

Jim Jackson, the author of *Christianomics*, gave his business assets of $6 million to the Lord. Afterwards, he realized the house he was living in was built with untithed money. He promised God to pay his tithe debt, but he asked God for help, since he had already given away his business assets. God answered Jim's prayers with an opportunity to buy some property, which he resold and made enough profit on to pay his tithe debt.

Jim now teaches the T.Y.E.N. (Tithing Your Estate Now) principle around the country. He is used by God to secure medical equipment and donate it to free clinics in Third World countries.

He also trains Third World religious leaders how to teach the Bible. Jim is living proof that tithing leads to financial victory.

THE TEMPTATION OF IDOLATRY

What causes a man to take his ax, cut down a tree, and use part of it for firewood and the leftover stump to carve a god? With his own knife and chisel, he forms a god he can touch. He then melts an old family silver necklace, bracelet, or bowl to molten metal to form hair, eyes and other features on his new god. The same man will place it in his home, bow down before it, and say, "You are my god." (See Isaiah 44:14–18.)

Blessed money is any money that has been tithed to God and used as He directs. It is the only real assurance for long-term financial victory.

This scenario may seem far-fetched in our modern, sophisticated, Western society. After all, we don't bow down to graven images and idols anymore, do we? Maybe we have invented other forms of idolatry that seem less pagan and primitive?

What is the purpose of idolatry? It is the need to hold an object in your hand in which you can place your faith. If you can somehow touch it, you receive instant gratification and a feeling of safety. It doesn't matter that you have just put your faith in a lie—your own creation. It is only important that you can touch it.

This happens every week in churches across the world when the offering plate is passed. Some put their faith in God and wait on Him to fulfill His promise to bless the tithe and offerings. Others hold their silver in their hands, keep it back, and put their faith only in what is in their hand. Their lack of faith to trust God with their 10 percent is indeed idolatry. Holding on to it seems to give them a sense of confidence that it will sustain them. They mistaken to think it is the thing that got them to where they are. These few coins become the object of their faith and worship; their purpose for living, to make more silver coins. In other words, they are carving out another false hope.

CONQUERING THE CANAANITES

PERSONAL EVALUATION & REFLECTION

Meditate on the following questions and answer them honestly.

1. How many people do you personally know who seem to be overcome with the love of money? Are they genuinely happy?

2. Ask yourself if you are living on dirty money. (See 1 Timothy 3:8.)

3. Be honest and ask yourself if you are a cheerful giver. (See 2 Corinthians 9:7.)

4. Do you tithe more than just money?

5. Read the story of how Achan brought a curse upon his entire house by stealing from God. (See Joshua 7.)

GROUP DISCUSSION

1. Discuss the difference between having money and loving money. Ask the question, "Is it okay to have money in the kingdom of God, or does He want to keep you poor in order to keep you humble?"

2. Discuss the process of how greed gets in.

3. Discuss the process of how to root out greed.

4. Discuss the tithe of Canaan—Jericho.

5. Discuss the concept of the love of money and how withholding the tithe constitutes idolatry.

GROUP EXERCISE

Ask someone in the group to give a testimony of how God has blessed him or her because of tithing.

chapter 15

CONQUERING THE HITTITES

OVERCOMING THE SPIRIT OF FEAR

Joshua said, "By this you shall know that the living God is among
you, and that He will without fail drive out from before you the
*Canaanites and **the Hittites** and the Hivites and the Perizzites*
and the Girgashites and the Amorites and the Jebusites."
(Joshua 3:10, emphasis added)

But if you do not drive out the inhabitants of the land from
before you, then it shall be that those whom you let remain shall
be irritants in your eyes and thorns in your sides, and they shall
harass you in the land where you dwell.   (Numbers 33:55)

J im Whittaker, the first American to reach the summit of Mount
Everest, said, "You never conquer a mountain. Mountains can't
be conquered; you conquer yourself—your hopes, your fears."
The word *Hittite* comes from the Hebrew word *chittiy*, which means
"terror."

Fear is Satan's favorite playground. Fear causes your blood pressure to rise, your heart to fail, your imagination to work overtime,
and your faith to falter. When Satan can't entice you, he tries to

scare you. If he can't lure you, he tries to manipulate you. He will only play if he can be the bully.

A THREEFOLD STRUGGLE WITH FEAR

Once again, mankind is a trinitarian being—body, soul, and spirit. Perhaps that is what God was referring to when He said, *"Let Us make man in Our image, according to Our likeness"* (Genesis 1:26). Because of the trinity of man, we struggle with fear on these three levels:

Physical Fear

First, we fear physical harm. Usually, this is a natural type of fear God gave us for our own survival and safety.

Soul Fear

Second, we struggle with emotional fears. This type of fear is manifested through worry, anxiety, and depression. Soul fear doesn't deal as much with actual threats as with potential or imaginary threats. This is where Satan wants to set up strongholds in our lives.

Spiritual Fear

Third, there is the spiritual side of fear. The *"spirit of fear"* causes us to lose faith in God and become more afraid of Satan than we are confident of God. The Bible addresses this in 2 Timothy 1:7: *"For God has not given us a spirit of fear, but of power and of love and of a sound mind."*

If you become entrapped by fear, you can lose your health, your talents, and your future. Fear is a thief that robs you of the quality of life. It can do the following:

- dominate the atmosphere of your home
- weaken your family

- fill your heart with such distrust that you have no faith
- ruin your Christian testimony

REGINA'S STORY

Regina (not her real name) came to me several years ago for counseling. On the outside, she was well-groomed, pleasant, and courteous. Inside, however, she suffered from debilitating panic attacks. She sought medical treatment, which made her life tolerable, but the attacks did not go away. Her doctor couldn't find any medical reason for the attacks, so he sent her to a psychiatrist. After intense counseling, medication was prescribed. It worked on the symptoms, but her fear never went away.

Finally, Regina came to me seeking spiritual advice for her situation. We discussed the progress she had made through her doctor, counselor, and medication. It seemed she was doing everything that could be done. However, she was still scared.

When I gave her a series of tests on her feelings about death, God, and herself, the true problem was revealed.

> *The* "spirit of fear" *causes us to lose faith in God and become more afraid of Satan than we are confident of God.*

She was healthy and reasonably stable, but her view of God was as someone who only punishes us. As it turned out, this was the basis of all her fears. Satan had deceived her into thinking he could bully her and she would be defenseless.

We did a study together on the character and nature of God and His attributes. Eventually, she was delivered of her abnormal fear. Today, she is pursuing God and is one of the most fervent worshippers I know. She now quotes the apostle Paul, who said,

"If God is for us, who can be against us?" (Romans 8:31). It's a basic fact: the more we fill our minds and hearts with God, the less room there is for fear.

The Remedy for Fear

The power of love is stronger than fear. First John 4:18 says, *"There is no fear in love; but perfect love casts out fear, because fear involves torment. But he who fears has not been made perfect in love."* God's love is the greatest power in the universe; it is the antidote to fear.

When His love is exemplified in our hearts, fear loses its power to reign. For love of a child, a father who is fearful will run into a burning building to rescue that child. Love will cause a parent who is terrified of water to jump into a pool to save a drowning child. Love for country and family will send soldiers to the horrors of a battlefield to insure freedom for future generations.

- Love says, "What can I do for others?"; fear says, "What can others do to me?"

- Love thinks no evil; fear dwells on evil thoughts.

- Love focuses on today's acts of kindness; fear focuses on tomorrow's uncertainties.

- Love leads to joy and peace; fear leads to distrust and defensiveness.

- Love reaches out to others; fear withdraws from others.

The principle is simple: the more we love, the less we fear!

Conquering the Hittites

What about the battle with the Hittites? It never occurred! The men of Israel allowed the Hittites to live in the land and did not drive them out as the Lord commanded. The Hittites continued to live in the land and began to intermarry with the Israelites throughout their residence in Canaan.

What was the problem? The problem wasn't a physical or mental threat—Israel's army was bigger and God had already promised them victory. The problem was spiritual. After all they had experienced, they still did not understand the enormity of God's provision. They chose to disobey God and allow the Hittites to remain on their Promised Land.

> *The bigger God is to us, the smaller everything else becomes. When we change our view of God, we will change whom we fear and what we fear.*

If we allow fear to remain, how can we accomplish everything God wants for us? Fear must be conquered!

The bigger God is to us, the smaller everything else becomes. We can never comprehend the depth, height, breadth, and length of God's love without first knowing Him. When we change our view of God, we will change whom we fear and what we fear.

CONQUERING THE HITTITES

PERSONAL EVALUATION & REFLECTION

Meditate on the following questions and answer them honestly.

1. What are your fears?
2. Are they bigger or more powerful than God?
3. Do you genuinely believe God loves you?
4. Are you willing to confront your fears by denouncing them out loud?
5. Are most of your fears based on the past, the present, or the future?

GROUP DISCUSSION

1. Discuss what it means to have a sound mind.
2. Discuss what it means to have a spirit of power and a spirit of love.
3. Discuss what you think the spirit of fear is.
4. Discuss God's love as the greatest power in the universe.
5. Discuss the outcome of the men of Israel allowing the Hittites to remain in their land.
6. Pray for anyone in the group who is dealing with fear.

GROUP EXERCISE

Ask someone in the group to give a testimony of overcoming fear.

chapter 16

CONQUERING THE HIVITES

OVERCOMING OUR DEPENDENCY ON THE WORLD

*Joshua said, "By this you shall know that the living God is among you, and that He will without fail drive out from before you the Canaanites and the Hittites and **the Hivites** and the Perizzites and the Girgashites and the Amorites and the Jebusites."*

(Joshua 3:10, emphasis added)

But if you do not drive out the inhabitants of the land from before you, then it shall be that those whom you let remain shall be irritants in your eyes and thorns in your sides, and they shall harass you in the land where you dwell. (Numbers 33:55)

T he story of the Hivites is recorded in Joshua 9:1–23. The kings of Canaan had gathered in a united effort to destroy their new enemy. Among those who assembled were the Hittites, the Amorites, the Canaanites, the Perizzites, the Hivites, and the Jebusites. These armies began to march onto the battlefield outside of Lebanon. Their arrival was announced with the thunderous roar of horses' hooves pounding the ground.

When the Hivites heard about the victories God had given Israel at Ai and Jericho, they sent ambassadors to make a covenant with Joshua. The Hivite parade made its way into the Israelite camp at Gilgal with their torn wineskins and moldy victuals. *"They said to Joshua, 'We are your servants.' And Joshua said to them, 'Who are you, and where do you come from?'"* (Joshua 9:8).

The Hivites lied and said,

> *From a very far country your servants have come, because of the name of the LORD your God; for we have heard of His fame, and all that He did in Egypt....This bread of ours we took hot for our provision from our houses on the day we departed to come to you. But now look, it is dry and moldy. And these wineskins which we filled were new, and see, they are torn; and these our garments and our sandals have become old because of the very long journey.* (Joshua 9:9, 12–13)

Without consulting the Lord or the elders of Israel, Joshua promised to be their ally.

Three days later, Joshua learned he had been deceived. He went to the camp of the Hivites but was forbidden from destroying them. He had taken an oath before the Lord that the people with whom they had made covenants would not be hurt. The princes of Israel were angered by this deception and decided that even though they had to let the Hivites live, they would enslave them.

NOT FOR SALE

Have you ever driven around a neighborhood looking for a sign that read, FOR SALE? It's funny to me that I have never seen a sign that read, NOT FOR SALE. The fact is: if you have a price, Satan will meet it.

Several years ago, Hollywood produced the film *Indecent Proposal,* in which a handsome millionaire offers a young couple $1 million to spend one night with the man's wife. Upon the film's release, talk show hosts were asking the question, "Are you for sale?"

The consensus was that most people are not for sale when the price is low. However, the higher the price gets, the more they are inclined to think about it and perhaps accept any type of offer. There is no difference in a $20 prostitute and a $1 million prostitute. The only question is the price.

The question every child of God must answer is this: Do you have a price at which you will forsake God? It's easy to say no, until the offer is made. If you have a price, Satan will either meet it or he will make you *believe* he will meet it.

> *If you have a price, Satan will either meet it or he will make you believe he will meet it.*

Teenagers need to stand up in the face of enticing offers of sex, drugs, popularity, and money, and say, "I am not for sale." Adults need to stand up in the face of enticing offers of sex, money, entertainment, prestige, and power, and say, "I am not for sale." The only answer to the question "Are you for sale?" is "No! Not to anyone; not for any price; not for any reason."

MAKING A DEAL WITH THE DEVIL

Connie was raised in a good family. She went on summer vacations with her parents and brothers. From all appearances, she was a normal sixteen-year-old girl in the youth group at church.

Connie's boyfriend Greg wasn't quite so fortunate. His only parent was an alcoholic mother. Greg raised himself most of his life. He continued to press Connie for more affection and physical contact. She knew she could only give herself to the man she married and had planned to save herself for that day. Connie's youth pastor tried to reason with her about dating a boy who was not a believer, but she replied, "Maybe I can help him."

Greg continued to push until he finally convinced her to compromise her standards. Greg and Connie's promiscuous relationship eventually led to other things. Before Connie realized it, Greg was arranging for her to sleep with several of his friends. This led to camping trips with many boys and just Connie. She never thought she would succumb to such degradation—but she had already said yes.

Soon, Connie learned she was pregnant. She decided to tell her parents and have the baby. Three months into the pregnancy, the doctor found a problem. Since the boy who fathered Connie's baby was a drug user, the baby suffered from severe disfigurement. Connie's baby was born blind, with no left arm, and partially paralyzed; the child also would never be able to speak.

For the first time, Connie realized that when you open a window of opportunity to the devil you never know what else you are letting in. Not only did she hurt herself, but she also brought a great burden upon her family. Connie's baby lived seven years. Connie never finished high school or attended college. Today she also is a drug addict who lives with one or two men every year. She never thought it could happen to her, but she discovered that deals with the devil are never what they appear.

What in the World Do You Want?

The word *Hivite*, or *Chivviy* in Hebrew, which derives from the word *Chavvah*, meaning "village," and also "a life giver." It speaks of living in a community or village and depending on the village for life. Even though community is important, a village is only as good as its god.

Do not love the world or the things in the world. If anyone loves the world, the love of the Father is not in him. For all that is in the world; the lust of the flesh, the lust of the eyes, and the pride of life; is not of the Father but is of the world. (1 John 2:15–16)

We are in the world, but we are not of this world. The temptation to look to the world for our sustenance is the Hivite compact.

God's plan for our lives starts with dependence on Him. Too many people have "sold their souls" in order to run in popular circles where they can be successful and powerful. This is the system of this world. The government of God is one of servitude, denying self, and taking up our cross to follow Christ. God will exalt us in His time, but we must do things God's way.

> *The temptation to look to the world instead of to God for our sustenance is the Hivite compact.*

SHORTCUTS TO SUCCESS

True champions do what they hate now so they can do what they love later. They do not believe in shortcuts. True champions know that shortcuts today affect the quality of tomorrow. We can't afford to exchange quality for quantity. Quantity follows quality, but quality does not always follow quantity.

At the end of his life, Solomon wrote the book of Ecclesiastes. He summed up the meaning of happiness when he said,

> *Go, eat your bread with joy, and drink your wine with a merry heart....Live joyfully with the wife whom you love all the days.... Whatever your hand finds to do, do it with your might.*
>
> (Ecclesiastes 9:7, 9–10)

In other words, "Enjoy your food, fall in love, and enjoy your work." Solomon said that everything else in life is like chasing after the wind. People who sell out early to this world's system often find they have spent their lives chasing the wind. Doing more things will not always make you more productive—it usually only makes you busier.

DINAH AND THE HIVITE

When we decide to make our own decisions without the guidance of the Holy Spirit, we are endangering the lives of future generations. Even if we find our way back, there is no guarantee the next generation will do the same.

Genesis 34 tells the story of Dinah and the Hivite. Jacob fathered twelve sons whose descendents would one day be known as the twelve tribes of Israel. Jacob was so proud of his sons, but he also loved his daughter, Dinah. She, however, went off on her own—not the usual behavior of an unmarried woman at the time. That's where she met Shechem, the prince of the Hivites. But Shechem did not have the same values as Dinah. Soon he drew this daughter of Jacob into his web of selfish intent where *"he took her and lay with her, and violated her"* (Genesis 34:2).

It was a different culture with a different value system, and no one did anything to help Dinah. Perhaps it was her handmaiden who ran back to tell Jacob that his daughter had been defiled. Soon, Shechem lay dead by the swords of Simeon and Levi, Dinah's brothers. Her other brothers arrived with their servants and slew the entire city in retaliation for the violation of their sister Dinah.

You cannot flirt with sin! You cannot swoon at worldly enticements, lest they become thorns to you and your household in due time.

Conquering the Hivites

Personal Evaluation & Reflection

Meditate on the following questions and answer them honestly.

1. What areas of your life are Not for Sale?

2. Do you have a price tag on your faith?

3. What area of your life tempts you or pulls you toward the world?

4. Is there anyone in your life who is luring you into the world?

5. Was there ever a time in your life when you were being pulled back to the world? What kept you from going back?

Group Discussion

1. Read and discuss I John 2:15-17.

2. Discuss Solomon's conclusion to the meaning of success and happiness.

   • To enjoy food.

   • To fall in love.

   • To enjoy your work.

3. Discuss some of the lures and enticements Satan uses to pull us back into the world.

4. Discuss the Hivite compact and its consequences.

5. As a group, put together a plan to continually
   overcome the world.

6. Ask the group if there is a person in their lives
   they could trust to discuss their struggles with
   temptation and pray with them.

7. Discuss what you should do if you have already
   succumbed to the temptation of the world in
   some area.

GROUP EXERCISE

Ask someone in the group who has succumbed to the
enticement of the world to give his or her testimony. What did
he or she discover? To whom did he or she turn for encouragement and strength?

chapter 17

CONQUERING THE PERIZZITES

OVERCOMING EMOTIONAL PARASITES

*Joshua said, "By this you shall know that the living God is among you, and that He will without fail drive out from before you the Canaanites and the Hittites and the Hivites and **the Perizzites** and the Girgashites and the Amorites and the Jebusites."* (Joshua 3:10, emphasis added)

But if you do not drive out the inhabitants of the land from before you, then it shall be that those whom you let remain shall be irritants in your eyes and thorns in your sides, and they shall harass you in the land where you dwell. (Numbers 33:55)

Have you ever had a bad feeling you couldn't describe? Perhaps you simply felt that something wasn't right but you thought, *I just can't put my finger on it.* One of the hardest things in our lives to conquer is that ambiguous, obscure emotion that hides below the surface in our subconscious just waiting to resurface at the wrong time like a bad dream. This is exactly how the nomadic Perizzites operated.

The Perizzites were nomadic tribes that lived among the people of Canaan. They got their name from their homesteading trait of living in unwalled villages. This was one of the most difficult groups of all to conquer because they were so mobile. How do you plan an attack on someone who may pull up stakes and leave at any time? Who are they? Where do they come? How did they get there in the first place?

The genealogy of this group is never mentioned in the Bible, but historians speculate that they were infused from members of many of the Canaanite tribes that chose to leave a life of discipline, government, and rule to wander the desert as free spirits. Because they came from various groups and armies, this gave them a military advantage. Like the minutemen of the colonial America, these nomads waged unconventional warfare. While the minutemen hid behind rocks and trees, the English redcoats lined up in neat formation and ranks, becoming easy prey for the amateur yet sharpshooting marksmen. This unconventional approach to battle won the colonies their freedom and made them a threatening enemy. Likewise, these free-ranging Perizzites became dangerous to larger, more disciplined armies who fought against them.

A PERIZZITE OR A PARASITE?

In the spiritual realm, the Perizzites represent hidden sins—unresolved conflict and festering unforgiveness that hide beneath the layers of our thoughts, will, and emotions. Like the Perizzites, they surface when we least expect them, showing up in the form of distorted feelings and emotions that are difficult to describe. They can ruin our day with unexpected attacks against our attitude. They wreak havoc on our relationships with harsh words that come out of our mouths in moments of stress. Before self-control can rise up and prevent the collateral damage, someone we care about is already wounded by a surprise attack from the hidden enemy that lurks camouflaged beneath our emotions. We may think, *I didn't even know I felt that way*, or, *Where did that come from?* Like an undetected parasite in your body that drains you of vital nutrients and good health, these Perizzites eat away at your soul until you are emotionally malnourished and unhealthy.

An Unexpected Visit by the Holy Spirit

I was attending a prayer conference many years ago and was especially excited about hearing Dr. Raymond Culpepper, a great pastor and noted speaker. As Dr. Culpepper began his presentation, I realized his subject matter was one of the most familiar subjects in Christendom: the Lord's Prayer. At first, I was a little disappointed because he was noted for digging gold out of biblical passages, and I was looking for something with a little more depth. I thought this was going to be "just another sermon." I was wrong.

As he began to dissect these verses, I found myself on a spiritual journey. Eventually he got to Matthew 6:12–13: *"Forgive us our debts, as we forgive our debtors. And do not lead us into temptation, but deliver us from the evil one."* Immediately, I found myself face-to-face with an unexpected visit by the Holy Spirit. Dr. Culpepper began to describe how unforgiveness in our past can lead us into present temptation. Those debts, or trespasses, lead us like a ghostly guide into temptation, where we make choices that we never would have made if we had only dealt

> *In the spiritual realm, the Perizzites represent hidden sins—unresolved conflict and festering unforgiveness that hide beneath the layers of our thoughts, will, and emotions.*

with them. Even though I couldn't think of a single person whom I needed to forgive or make restitution with, I clearly heard the Holy Spirit say, "take the journey." I never dreamed that this cleansing process would take me more than two years to complete.

My method was straightforward. I simply went before the Lord every day and said, "Forgive me my debts as I forgive my debtors. Lord, show me my debts and my debtors." I would wait quietly in His presence as He took me on the journey of my life and began to reveal people with whom I had gotten angry, yet had never resolved the issue. Instead, I moved on and left them out of my life while still hanging on to the resentment. What I didn't realize was that, for much of my life, I had been making some poor decisions based on my woundedness over these broken relationships.

One of those individuals was a family member who had stolen an heirloom from me. When my grandfather died, I was given an antique, single shot, octagon-barreled rifle as a keepsake. I valued it more as a sentimental connection with my grandfather than as a material possession. While I was away at college, a member of our extended family took the rifle from my closet and pawned it. By the time I found out, it was months later, and there was nothing I could do about it. When I confronted this person, he denied it, but we found the paperwork that proved he had taken it to the pawn shop. Despite my efforts, I was not able to trace down my grandfather's gift to me. I was angry for a long time, but eventually I moved on and never spoke of it again. Eventually, I relocated to Missouri and allowed the span of space and time to be a substitute for actually dealing with the issue.

While God worked with me on my "debts," He reminded me of this hidden anger that I had buried. This Perizzite in my spirit was causing me to be suspicious of other people in my life and disabling my ability to trust. I had no idea that this hurtful event, long buried in my past, was still leading me into temptation. I knew that if I confronted this person now, years later, he would only deny it again, and others would say, "Why do you have to bring that up again? It was such a long time ago. Why can't you just let it go?" I also knew that without closure it was still within me, waiting to explode like an emotional land mine. No amount of passing time would be able to erase that nomadic enemy within my soul. I had to kill the Perizzite. I had to forgive and release this issue permanently.

I asked God to guide me in how to deal with this. In my spirit, He instructed me to write the family member a check for the amount the gun had been pawned for. This would let him know I had the proof of what he had done. The rest was up to him. If he repented, we could rebuild our relationship. Even if he didn't, however, I would have done everything in my power to release it.

> *Unforgiven debts or trespasses lead us like a ghostly guide into temptation, where we make choices that we never would have made if we had only dealt with them.*

I sent the check with a brief note, not really sure how he would respond. I waited for over a month with no response. Finally I received the cancelled check from my bank indicating that he had endorsed and cashed the check. There was no moment of restitution. This person was not a Christian, and his heart was too hard to ask for forgiveness. Instead, he simply cashed the check and never mentioned it. No note, no phone call, nothing but the name on the back of my check.

Amazingly, even without his apology, I was still set free. This is the first time I have ever written about it, but ever since that day when I saw the cancelled check, I was free of any anger or unforgiveness.

The nomadic warrior who lurked in the layers of my soul was found and expelled.

THE ANGEL OF PROMISE

Behold, I send an angel before you to keep you in the way and to bring you into the place which I have prepared....For My angel will go before you and bring you in to the Amorites and the Hittites and the Perizzites and the Canaanites and the Hivites and the Jebusites; and I will cut them off. You shall not bow down to their gods, nor serve them, nor do according to their works; but you shall utterly overthrow them and completely break down their sacred pillars. So you shall serve the LORD your God, and He will bless your bread and your water. And I will take sickness away from the midst of you. (Exodus 23:20, 23–25)

When the Lord initially sent the children of Israel to the land of promise, He sent them in with a guide. This guide was an angel assigned to bring them into their inheritance. It specifically mentions that this angel would show them where the Perizzites were hidden and would reveal the ways to *"cut them off."* The passage indicates that these enemies must be overthrown or else the Israelites would *"serve them"* and *"do their works,"* allowing these enemies to establish *"sacred pillars"* in their lives. Lastly, the passage promises that if the Israelites would serve the Lord, He would bless them and remove their sicknesses from among them. Similarly, hidden Perizzites in your emotional life can cause you to do their work, allowing them to set up sacred pillars of sin and sickness in your body.

Spirits of oppression in your life cannot operate without entry points. These low ranking spirits are expert liars, attacking your spirit through the power of suggestion. Remember the cartoon with the angel on one shoulder and the devil on the other? That is a good picture of the spirit of oppression. They suggest things that discourage you and oppress your emotions. They may dredge up past scenes from your life that caused you pain. This is subconscious information that was never filed away properly. If we fail to reveal and close out these moments in time, the oppressors will bring them up at the most inconvenient time and prod you to do "their work."

If oppressive spirits find that there is no warfare against them and they can operate freely, they will set up their "sacred pillars." These pillars mark their territory. They are like a sign on an office door that tells you who works there. It is a symbolic presence of the oppressor that has now become a part of your attitude, personality, and decision-making mechanism. You now base your opinions and choices based on how you *feel*, but who is controlling how you feel? That's right; it's a "Perizzite."

I believe that unforgiveness, lack of closure, and hidden anger can make you sick and open up doors for disease within your body. Every day our bodies ingest things that could potentially be harmful to us, but our strong immune systems fight them off. A body weakened by stress, restlessness, lack of joy, and lack of peace is subject to sickness much more than an individual in good spiritual, mental, and physical health.

> *A body weakened by stress, restlessness, lack of joy, and lack of peace is subject to sickness much more than an individual in good spiritual, mental, and physical health.*

We must allow God's angels and the power of the Holy Spirit to reveal the presence of "Perizzites" in our life and help us to get rid of them. In my experience, this will not happen with the kind of prayer in which we do all the talking. It will only happen in a quiet place where you can become still before the Lord and go into the past places of your life to look behind those long ago closed doors. This is not an event; it's a journey.

In my two year process of praying the Lord's Prayer, I uncovered almost twenty events that had negatively influenced my life—events that I had never dealt with. I had to write some letters, make some phone calls, and ask a few people to forgive me. I called up an old friend and asked him to forgive me for holding something against him for over twenty years. He didn't even know about it. He knew we no longer spoke, but didn't know why. He actually got on a plane to come and see me. Today, we are close friends once again, and he is one of my treasured confidants. Each time "the angel" would guide me to another hidden place, I always thought it was the last one. Sometimes it would take weeks for me to find the next one, and sometimes I would find several at once. Eventually the searchlight of my soul was able to give me a total freedom from the enemies hiding in my emotions—enemies that I hadn't even known existed. For the first time, I was able to taste milk and honey without looking over my shoulder and feeling guilty for being so blessed.

Conquering the Perizzites

Personal Evaluation & Reflection

Meditate on the following questions and answer them honestly.

1. Do you ever find yourself snapping at people for no reason and wondering where your short temper came from?

2. Is there any collateral damage in your life—"innocent" people who have suffered your emotional attacks due to something or someone else from your past?

3. Does anyone or anything come to mind when you examine your life for unresolved conflict?

Group Discussion

1. Discuss the unconventional warfare of the Perizzites and how that compares to the surprising way our emotions can launch an attack.

2. Discuss the ways in which lingering anger and unforgiveness can lead to sickness in our physical bodies.

3. Ask someone in the group to share how an unresolved conflict in his or her life affected him or her years later—and what, if anything, he or she did about it.

GROUP EXERCISE

Have the group spend time in silence, allowing the Holy Spirit to reveal any past areas of anger or unforgiveness long forgotten that may still be affecting their attitudes and emotions to this day. Take time to have the group pray for each person to be delivered and achieve freedom from the Perizzites hidden in his or her soul. If someone has had trouble identifying any, pray for him or her to be able to continue the journey of self-examination in the coming week.

chapter 18

CONQUERING THE GIRGASHITES

OVERCOMING THE FEAR OF THE WORLD

*Joshua said, "By this you shall know that the living God is among you, and that He will without fail drive out from before you the Canaanites and the Hittites and the Hivites and the Perizzites and **the Girgashites** and the Amorites and the Jebusites."*
(Joshua 3:10, emphasis added)

But if you do not drive out the inhabitants of the land from before you, then it shall be that those whom you let remain shall be irritants in your eyes and thorns in your sides, and they shall harass you in the land where you dwell. (Numbers 33:55)

D o some of these statements seem familiar to you at all? Are you rewinding the tape and replaying them in your mind?

- "Look what you could have had by now!"
- "If only you had married someone else."
- "You should have stayed where you were."
- "If only you had listened!"

The word *Girgashite* comes from a Hebrew word that means "turning back." The spirit of the Girgashites calls out, "Go back! Give up on your dream. Start over again. God has let you down. Egypt was better than this."

> **The good news is that even people with a long history of bad behavior patterns are able to change.**

The enticements of yesterday often seem sweeter than the bitterness of today. There are several things we must do to resist the pull of the world. First, we must get away from our present situation in order to think more clearly. It's amazing how distorted life looks when we only look at part of the picture. Second, we must move to higher ground in order to see the big picture. Third, we must seek wise counsel from someone who will tell us the truth. Finally, we must allow the Holy Spirit to show us the way past the temptation. There is always a way out when God is our guide. (See 1 Corinthians 10:13.)

WALKING OUT ON GOD FOR THE LAST TIME

Jimmy's (not his real name) story is all too real. His musical giftings surpassed those of anyone I had ever seen, but his Christian walk was unstable. He was surrounded by godly people who loved him and prayed for him, but the pull of sin was too strong. The Girgashite spirit whispered his name like a whistling wind in the night. No matter how far away from the world he seemed to get, he always ran back for one more taste, one more look, one more night of fun. Each time was supposed to be the last.

The cycle continued for years. We wanted to believe Jimmy would change, but his track record was a long and discouraging one. One day it finally happened—Jimmy slammed the door on sin and never strayed again. At first, I couldn't figure out what made the difference. On the surface, it seemed like all the other times, but now the look in his eyes was different. His questions were different; his jokes were different. It became obvious to the bleachers full of skeptics that this time he might just make it. Indeed he did! He had walked out on God for the last time.

This incident occurred years ago, and Jimmy is still going strong. His is a real success story for those being courted by the Girgashites. He stayed, he fought, and he won. This time, he finally went for depth, not breadth. Jimmy secured his foundation before he started using his gift again. His focus was no longer music, but God. The good news is that even people with a long history of bad behavior patterns are able to change.

WHY SOME GO BACK

Why do some walk out on God? There is a simple answer to this question: they lack depth. In Mark, we find the parable of the sower and the formula for why some walk out.

1. They Have No Depth in the Word of God

Listen! Behold, a sower went out to sow. And it happened, as he sowed, that some seed fell by the wayside; and the birds of the air came and devoured it. Some fell on stony ground, where it did not have much earth; and immediately it sprang up because it had no depth of earth. (Mark 4:3–5)

Some people exist on a junk-food diet of warmed-over sermons, stories of last year's revival, and feel-good theology that fails to take them deep enough in the Word of God.

The problem of biblical illiteracy is far too common in the body of Christ. Pews are filled with Christians who can give you the latest numbers on Wall Street, the most detailed sports statistics, and the latest happenings in the lives of Hollywood celebrities, but many of those same individuals can't quote one Scripture from the Word of God.

The first chapter of Ruth tells the story of a family that, during a time of famine, left *Bethlehem*, meaning "house of bread," and moved to *Moab*, meaning "cursed." The only real reason people go back to "cursed" is that there is no bread in the "House of Bread." New Christians can't survive on a stale diet—they need a fresh feast from the Bread of Life to sustain them.

2. They Have No Roots

When the sun was up it was scorched, and because it had no root it withered away. (Mark 4:6)

A new plant without a good root system will die from a lack of water supply and an overexposure to the heat. In short, it will wither.

Dried up in the pew. What a thought! The roots of Christianity come from a sound doctrine that anchors us to the foundation—Jesus. Yet we should heed the ominous warning of the apostle Paul:

The time will come when they will not endure sound doctrine, but according to their own desires, because they have itching ears.... (2 Timothy 4:3)

Entertaining sermons will never replace sound doctrine. Sermons can be funny, enjoyable, and exciting, but they must convey the irrefutable truths of Bible doctrine.

3. Without Roots, They Have No Endurance

They have no root in themselves, and so endure only for a time. (Mark 4:17)

A lack of depth causes some to be easily offended. Even though discipleship is important, we must not forget character. Education is great, but it will not make us wise. It will only make us more knowledgeable. Prosperity is wonderful, but it can only make us richer. These things don't change our character.

Intermingled with Jesus' spiritual lesson from the sower parable is His reminder that each person must be committed to personal character. We must know, like, and believe in ourselves in order to have depth. People with depth are secure. Those who live on surface emotions and relationships are often running from something. Their insecurity makes them easily offended and is ultimately what turns them back to the world.

✍. They Are Entangled with Thorns

Some seed fell among thorns; and the thorns grew up and choked it, and it yielded no crop. (Mark 4:7)

Jesus interpreted *"thorns"* as the cares of life, the deceitfulness of riches, and the lusts of life:

The ones sown among thorns; they are the ones who hear the word, and the cares of this world, the deceitfulness of riches, and the desires for other things entering in choke the word, and it becomes unfruitful. (Mark 4:18–19)

These are people who have one foot in the world and one foot in the church. They haven't truly committed to the kingdom of God.

All men struggle with sin in one area or another, but there is a difference between *struggling against* the flesh and *walking in* the flesh. It's the "flesh walk" and the "flesh talk" that pull many back to their old lifestyles.

THE DEBATE

The apostle Paul wrote, *"For the weapons of our warfare are not carnal but mighty in God for pulling down strongholds, casting down arguments"* (2 Corinthians 10:4–5).

> *Those who live on surface emotions and relationships are insecure, which makes them easily offended and is ultimately what turns them back to the world.*

Paul was referring to the great debates, where one man speaks and another rebuts. This argument or debate continues until one opponent begins to wear down the other. When he sees that his opponent is weak, he goes in with the final argument that ends and wins the debate. It is the lawyer's final argument that turns the heart of the jury. It is the politician's finest hour in a debate that wins him the election. We too are engaged in an argument. Our minds war with the "Girgashite spirit" on the subject of staying or going back. The battle rages:

Good says, "Deny yourself, take up your cross, and follow Jesus."

Evil snarls, "Gratify yourself, take up your lusts, and follow no man."

Evil continues, "You have rights; you deserve it; look what they did to you."

Good rebuts, "You have responsibilities; look what's been done for you."

Evil interrupts, "But imagine what you are missing."

Good comes back, "But look what you've gained."

Evil slams back, "But if you live for yourself, you can have many pleasures."

Good replies, "But if you live for God, you can have hope in this world and in the world to come."

Evil speaks, "But think of the fun."

Good replies, "Think of eternity."

Evil returns, "Think of the power."

Good rebuts, "Think of the love, joy and peace."

Evil repeats himself, "Think of the pleasure."

Good, realizing Evil is out of ideas, comes back, "Think of your purpose in life."

Evil stumbles over words and manages to stutter out, "Think of the p-p p-p-pleasure."

Good finishes with the winning statement, "No! Think of the joy unspeakable that is full of glory, the glory that does not fade away, the crown of life, the eternal citizenship in the city of God, the healing for your body, the peace for your mind, the forgiveness for your sins, the grace for your struggles, the mercy for your past, the deliverance for your soul, and the fruit of the Spirit for your character.

"Think of the prayer for your needs, the worship for your spirit, the Word of God for your road map, the Holy Spirit for your guide, Jesus for your King, God for your Father, heaven for your home, security for your future, destiny for your existence, angels for your protection, love for your marriage, truth for your stature, beauty for your eyes, music for your ears, peace for your home, blessings for your children, and power for your daily living."

End of argument!

CONQUERING THE GIRGASHITES

PERSONAL EVALUATION & REFLECTION

Meditate on the following questions and answer them honestly.

1. What negative message has the enemy sent you, tempting you to turn back?

2. Have you ever contemplated "going back" to the world? Why?

3. Do you feel you have a "big picture" of your life?

4. Do you have an honest person in your life who will speak the truth to you?

5. Do you feel you are founded in sound doctrine?

GROUP DISCUSSION

1. Discuss the issue of backsliding. What is the process? How subtly does it happen? What are the signs that someone is backsliding?

2. Discuss these two questions:
   • Why do people go back?
   • Why do people stay?

3. Ask members of the group to share how they deal with the "cares of life" to say strong spiritually.

4. What can the church do to get more people rooted in the Word of God?

5. Discuss the importance of a "made-up" mind in serving God.

GROUP EXERCISE

Ask the group to share testimonies of people who overcame the pull of the world.

chapter 19

CONQUERING THE AMORITES

OVERCOMING THE SPIRIT OF CRITICISM

*Joshua said, "By this you shall know that the living God is among you, and that He will without fail drive out from before you the Canaanites and the Hittites and the Hivites and the Perizzites and the Girgashites and **the Amorites** and the Jebusites."*
                                                     (Joshua 3:10, emphasis added)

But if you do not drive out the inhabitants of the land from before you, then it shall be that those whom you let remain shall be irritants in your eyes and thorns in your sides, and they shall harass you in the land where you dwell.   (Numbers 33:55)

F oreigners often make us uncomfortable. Who are they? What do they eat? Why do they wear that? What do they do all day long? Are they like us? God's ominous warning to the children of Israel about all the Canaanite nations in Numbers 3:55 was never so alarming as it was when they met their first Amorite. God said that if they did not drive the enemy out of the land, the Amorites would become irritants in their eyes and thorns in their sides.

What was wrong with the Amorites? Wouldn't the best approach be to convert them rather than run them out? We learn from the story of Ruth, the Moabitess, that God did not have a problem with the *people* of these nations; after all, Ruth became a part of the lineage of Christ. So why did God want to run them out?

The problem wasn't with them; it was with their beliefs in their strange gods. God knew that in order to someday reach these strange people, the children of Israel must first become established.

The application for us is that we, as Christians, should never try to rescue other people when we ourselves need rescuing. Unless we are firmly established in our faith, dabbling with the beliefs of another person may only lead us into confusion. We must be grounded before challenging the beliefs of others.

> *Idle words bring confusion and death. Bridled words bring peace and life. Our words are the sword of our spirit; they start and end our personal battles.*

The word *Amorite* comes from the root word *amar*, meaning "to say, to challenge, to charge, or to speak against." Words have power. They can throw a nation into chaos, destroy a family, start a war, sentence someone to life in prison, command an army, elect a politician, or even lead a nation.

God spoke the world into existence. (See Genesis 1.) Likewise, we who were created in the image of God have the ability to influence our individual worlds by what we speak. The words you speak impact the life you lead.

Amorites were known for their critical nature. They were masters of debate and argument. The danger of the Amorite nation was not their ability to use a sword and spear, but their persuasiveness. They used the power of influence and debate through crafty words to rule, manipulate, and control their world.

IDLE WORDS AND BRIDLED WORDS

What does the Bible say about words?

I say to you that for every idle word men may speak, they will give account of it in the day of judgment. (Matthew 12:36)

Indeed, we put bits in horses' mouths that they may obey us, and we turn their whole body. Look also at ships: although they are so large and are driven by fierce winds, they are turned by a very small rudder wherever the pilot desires. Even so the tongue is a little member and boasts great things. See how great a forest a little fire kindles! (James 3:3–5)

The Bible distinctly speaks of two types of words—idle words and bridled words. Idle words bring confusion and death. Bridled words bring peace and life. *"Death and life are in the power of the tongue"* (Proverbs 18:21). Our words are the sword of our spirit; they start and end our personal battles.

MOSES AND THE AMORITE SPIRIT

The Amorite spirit has always been around. Not only did Moses physically defeat the giant Amorite king, Og (see Deuteronomy 3:1–11), he also had his own personal battle with the Amorite spirit of criticism.

The pressure was mounting. The people were asking too many questions. We are more vulnerable to temptation and more likely to speak our minds when we feel tired and stressed—and Moses' stress was off the charts.

The Israelites cried out,

Why have you made us come up out of Egypt, to bring us to this evil place? It is not a place of grain or figs or vines or pomegranates; nor is there any water to drink. (Numbers 20:5)

The hot sun of the wilderness had parched their lips and made them weary. But none felt the heat like Moses. Not only did he have to find water, but he also had to get them to Canaan. Soon a murmuring riot of words broke out. Each complaint was a dagger in Moses' heart.

Satan's greatest temptations often come just before God's blessings. How does Satan know when God is going to bless? Because he sees the spiritual warfare that is fought in the heavenly realm. When Satan loses the battle against God's angelic army, he immediately sends hindering spirits to cause us to reject God's blessing.

Moses and Aaron gathered the congregation before a great rock. Moses' instruction from God was to speak to the rock and it would provide water. (See verse 8.)

[Moses] *said to them, "Hear now, you rebels! Must we bring water for you out of this rock?" Then Moses lifted his hand and struck the rock twice with his rod; and water came out abundantly, and the congregation and their animals drank.* (Numbers 20:10–11)

In this moment of weakness, Moses committed the offense that would keep him from entering Canaan. His act of disobedience seems like such a small thing. It seems that God may have judged him harshly, but the truth is revealed in the New Testament.

All passed through the sea, all were baptized into Moses in the cloud and in the sea, all ate the same spiritual food, and all drank the same spiritual drink. For they drank of that spiritual Rock that followed them, and that Rock was Christ.

(1 Corinthians 10:1–4)

That rock was the symbolic representation of Jesus Christ. Jesus Himself brought refreshing and sustaining water to the Israelites, and Moses "hit" Him. Not only did he strike his Savior, but he also turned on the people and yielded to the Amorite spirit. He yelled at them, *"Hear now, you rebels! Must we bring water for you out of this rock?"*

Years later, David would write a song about this incident:

They angered Him also at the waters of strife, so that it went ill with Moses on account of them; because they rebelled against His Spirit, so that he spoke rashly with his lips.

(Psalm 106:32–33)

This one lapse in judgment, this one loss of self-control in the face of criticism, derailed the ministry of Moses. As far as his mission of leading Israel into the Promised Land went, that was over. Moses would retire and die on the hill overlooking his goal. Our critics may be dead wrong in their opinions and in their methods of voicing them, but that is no excuse for us to forget who we are and let our emotions get the best of us.

ZACHARIAS AND THE AMORITE

The story of a priest named Zacharias, the father of John the Baptist, is recorded in Luke. When the angel told him of the child his wife would bear, he too yielded to the Amorite spirit by questioning the angel.

"Do not be afraid, Zacharias, for your prayer is heard; and your wife Elizabeth will bear you a son, and you shall call his name

233

John."...And Zacharias said to the angel, "How shall I know this? For I am an old man, and my wife is well advanced in years." And the angel answered and said to him, "I am Gabriel, who stands in the presence of God, and was sent to speak to you and bring you these glad tidings. But behold, you will be mute and not able to speak until the day these things take place, because you did not believe my words which will be fulfilled in their own time." (Luke 1:13, 18–20)

When John was born, the family asked about his name. Elizabeth said, "John." The neighbors and relatives thought it should be a family name. What did the father say?

So they made signs to his father; what he would have him called. And he asked for a writing tablet, and wrote, saying, "His name is John." So they all marveled. Immediately his mouth was opened and his tongue loosed, and he spoke, praising God.
(verses 62–64)

Immediately Zacharias' mouth was opened and he began to prophesy good things after this "fast of words." Perhaps if we went on a "word fast" we too would not yield to the temptation of the Amorite spirit so quickly.

CONQUERING THE AMORITE

Therefore the five kings of the Amorites, the king of Jerusalem, the king of Hebron, the king of Jarmuth, the king of Lachish, the king of Eglon, gathered themselves together, and went up, they and all their hosts, and encamped before Gibeon, and made war against it....And the LORD discomfited them before Israel, and slew them with a great slaughter.
(Joshua 10:5, 10 KJV)

Discomfit means "to frustrate the plans of" or "to put into a state of perplexity." The clouds rolled in like black limousines bringing God's assassins. The charge was given and the elements obeyed. The temperature of the earth changed as God gave the command: *"the LORD cast down large hailstones from heaven on them as far as Azekah, and they died"* (verse 11).

This battle would be long remembered because, on this day, the sun stood still to light up the battlefield of the Israelites and the Amorites. (See verses 12–14.) All of Israel looked on as God beat the Amorites with His artillery of hailstones. Scripture says that after the Israelites won the battle, *"no one moved his tongue against any of the children of Israel"* (verse 21).

> *Our critics may be dead wrong in their opinions and in their methods of voicing them, but that is no excuse for us to forget who we are and let our emotions get the best of us.*

They had killed more that just flesh. They had won a battle against the principality that ruled the Amorite kingdom. The five kings escaped the battle scene but were later captured. When Joshua found them in hiding, he made a spectacle of them by having the captains of the men of war place their feet on the kings' necks. (See verse 24.)

He knew where the real problem was. It was the spirit that caused them to speak out against God's people. With this victory, Israel was one battle closer to living peacefully in Canaan.

CONQUERING THE AMORITES

PERSONAL EVALUATION & REFLECTION

Meditate on the following questions and answer them honestly.

1. Who is your worst critic? Have you prayed for him or her lately?

2. Do you struggle with being overly critical?

3. How many friends in your life do not bridle their tongues?

4. Who are your greatest encouragers? Have you told them lately how much they mean to you?

5. Did you learn how to criticize from another person?

GROUP DISCUSSION

1. Discuss the phrase "The words you speak impact the life you lead."

2. Discuss the difference between constructive and destructive criticism.

3. Have someone in the group give an example of a person they know who does a good job at bridling his or her tongue.

4. Discuss the spirit of the Amorite. Is it a battle of the mind or a spirit that we must conquer?

5. What is the difference between complaining, murmuring, and criticizing? Is it a progression, where one leads into the other?

6. Read aloud the description of the battle against the Amorites in Joshua 10:5-15. Discuss the details of this battle to gain better spiritual insight.

GROUP EXERCISE

Have each member of the group write a warfare prayer against the Amorite spirit of criticism. Have someone read his or her prayer aloud.

chapter 20

CONQUERING THE JEBUSITES

OVERCOMING THE LACK OF CARE
FOR OUR PHYSICAL BODIES

*Joshua said, "By this you shall know that the living God is among you, and that He will without fail drive out from before you the Canaanites and the Hittites and the Hivites and the Perizzites and the Girgashites and the Amorites and **the Jebusites**."*
(Joshua 3:10, emphasis added)

But if you do not drive out the inhabitants of the land from before you, then it shall be that those whom you let remain shall be irritants in your eyes and thorns in your sides, and they shall harass you in the land where you dwell. (Numbers 33:55)

The capital city of the Jebusite nation was called Jebus. Later on it would be changed to Jerusalem. The oldest name of this city was Salem. The first time we hear about Salem is in Genesis when Abraham meets Melchizedek, king of Salem. (See Genesis 14:18.)

The word *Jebusite,* from the Hebrew word *Yebuwciy,* means "trodden down or threshing place." *Salem,* or in Hebrew, *Shalem,* means "peaceful." *Melchizedek* means "king of righteousness." Thus, we have the city of peace ruled by the king of righteousness. This sounds like a good place to live. Although through the years, the name came to be called Jerusalem because of changes in modern Hebrew dialect, we still might say that the original meaning of the word *Jerusalem* (Jebus Salem) is a "trodden down city of peace."

> *Victorious living is not just a happy life—it is also a healthy life. A toxic body doesn't feel or act victorious.*

By Joshua's day, the conquered city of Jerusalem, the Jebusite capital, was no longer the "city of peace" ruled by Melchizedek. It was now the "trodden down city of peace" ruled by Adoni-Zedek, king of the Jebusites.

Joshua's battle with the Jebusites is actually the same battle we discussed last chapter when Joshua conquered the Amorites. Several kings in this area met at Gibeon to fight with Joshua and his army. They called for their Amorite allies and the five kings of the Amorites came down to fight with them. One of the armies there was that of the Jebusites. This was the very battle that conquered the city of Jerusalem for the nation Israel, although it would not be fully retained until King David's rule.

WHO IS KING OF JERUSALEM NOW?

Jerusalem would eventually become known as the Holy City, the capital of Palestine. It is the place where the temple of God would be and where people would come from all over to worship Jehovah.

This raises a question to the church. If Jerusalem represented the dwelling place of God in His temple during the time of Israel, and will again during the millennial reign of Christ, where is God's temple now?

Paul answered that question for us:

Do you not know that your body is the temple of the Holy Spirit who is in you, whom you have from God, and you are not your own? (1 Corinthians 6:19)

If we are the temple of God, we are the spiritual Jerusalem during the Gentile age. (See Luke 21:41.) We must ask these questions now about our own bodies: Who is the king of Jerusalem now? Do our bodies reflect the "city of peace" or the "trodden down and polluted city?"

HAPPY, BUT NOT HEALTHY

Victorious living is not just a happy life—it is also a healthy life. A toxic body doesn't feel or act victorious. An unhealthy body that has been neglected is usually in no position to say yes to opportunity.

Shelly (not her real name) lived a life that most would call "disconnected." If you gave her a typical spiritual litmus test, she would pass with flying colors. She never abused her body with drugs or alcohol; she never contracted a transmittable disease. Her lifestyle was above that, and she was the first to let you know it. She didn't call herself a preacher, but she was noted for her "Bible-thumping" and finger-pointing. She had a lot to say about issues concerning her interpretation of holy living. Her list of "thou shalt nots" was much longer than God's original ten.

Yet she seemed to overlook the one thing that no one else could overlook. She did her preaching from a gluttonous body in which toxins fueled wild mood swings that caused her to become irate. In short, she didn't practice what she preached. Sadly, it wasn't even her physique that made her testimony nil; it was her self-righteous and judgmental attitude that rendered her friendless. Shelly is a prime example of how poor health can make you an irritable person. Her struggle with an eating disorder made her angry and lonely.

There are many people who suffer from physical problems that cause them to be overweight or unhealthy. True conquerors rise above their fight by developing and maintaining positive attitudes. In this country of plenty, many people who are tired, unhealthy, and overweight are self-made gluttons. They just have never made the choice to conquer their own flesh.

CONQUERING THE FLESH

God deserves a portion of our lives so that we can be alone with Him in fellowship and worship.

In our spiritual battles, we also encounter "Jebusites" that pollute and demean our bodies—the temple of God. These pollutants eventually affect our souls and spirits.

Back in Salem, God gave us an example of how our bodies can be a "city of peace." In Genesis 14, Abram (later called Abraham) had come from a great battle. He was tired and worn out. On his way home he met a man who represents Jesus in the Old Testament—Melchizedek. This king refreshed Abram by offering him bread and wine. This story embodies the four principles of "self-care."

1. We Need to Rest between Battles (Genesis 14:18–20)

God wants us to pace ourselves, not live like we are robots. Instead of going directly into another battle, Abram took time to stop, reflect, worship, and rest. The lack of restful sleep, proper diet, exercise, and spiritual renewal may determine whether we win or lose our next spiritual battle. Abram's pause to worship was one of the secrets to his greatness. He knew how to take "selah time." In Hebrew, *selah* means, in effect, "pause, stop, and think." Without selah time, we never rejuvenate spiritually.

2. When Tired, We Are Vulnerable to the Traps of Satan (Genesis 14:21-24)

Not only did Melchizedek come out to meet Abram, but the king of Sodom came with him. Remember Sodom, the city God destroyed because of its wickedness? The king of Sodom tried to offer Abram a bribe.

That's when Satan entices us. He preys on tired, worn-out warriors because he knows that when we are feeling good, our faith is stronger. Therefore, he often waits like a lion in the bushes, waiting to pounce at the first weak moment.

3. Abraham Paid His Tithes to Melchizedek (Genesis 14:20)

Tithes represent God's portion. If you want a healthy body, don't forget God's portion of your life. Most of the time, tithes are referred to in a monetary sense, and rightly so. However, the tithe is the portion of your life that belongs to God.

A portion of our day belongs to God. If we serve God only with leftover time, we don't serve Him well. God deserves a portion of our lives so that we can be alone with Him in fellowship and worship.

4. The King of Salem Offered Abram Bread and Wine (Genesis 14:18)

This foreshadowing of Communion teaches us a valuable principle about conquering our flesh. Our body can't be whole without our spirit being renewed; the two go hand in hand. Spiritual

243

refreshment is necessary for victorious living. Fun, fellowship, and religion can never replace genuine spiritual refreshment.

POLLUTED JERUSALEM

To be truly victorious, we must be committed to physical fitness. Too many Christians live in poor health. Their gluttonous bodies demonstrate what the Bible says: *"Whose end is destruction, whose god is their belly, and whose glory is in their shame; who set their mind on earthly things"* (Philippians 3:19).

Gluttons are idol worshippers who carry their god around in their belly. Gluttony not only gives a poor testimony, but it also pollutes the temple of the Holy Spirit.

> *If we want to pursue the will of God and live in victory, we will need healthy minds and healthy bodies.*

God will not dwell in an unclean temple. Bodies ruled by the flesh are like polluted cities. Bodies ruled by immorality are like cities in bondage. We can't live victoriously in a city of pollution. We must subdue the Jebusite spirit and return to the city of peace. We have an obligation to our earthly temples. If we want to pursue the will of God and live in victory, we will need healthy minds and healthy bodies.

The apostle Paul wrote, *"I beseech you therefore, brethren, by the mercies of God, that you present your bodies a living sacrifice, holy, acceptable to God, which is your reasonable service"* (Romans 12:1). Again, he wrote to the Corinthian church, *"For you were bought at a price; therefore glorify God in your body and in your spirit, which are God's"* (1 Corinthians 6:20).

Wars against Your Soul

Peter said to subdue the *"lusts of the flesh"* (2 Peter 2:18) that war against your soul. When you are at war with your flesh, it will grieve you. If you have a defeated mind-set over your failures, you allow Satan to incapacitate you with guilt and low self-esteem, which cause you to be "trodden down"—living under condemnation.

Satan seeks to destroy the peace of God that once ruled your mind. Toxic bodies are seldom at peace. Bodies filled with impurities force the liver, heart, and lungs to work overtime. Tiredness, depression, loss of joy, and lack of motivation replace love, joy, and peace in the Holy Spirit.

Don't Stop Yet

Joshua defeated the Jebusite king. Later, David defeated the remnant of the Jebusites and ruled God's people from Jerusalem. God still rules from His holy temple. You can defeat the Jebusite spirit that is wearing your body down and you can place the King of Righteousness back on the throne of your heart.

May the God of peace Himself sanctify you completely; and may your whole spirit, soul, and body be preserved blameless at the coming of our Lord Jesus Christ. (1 Thessalonians 5:23)

CONQUERING THE JEBUSITES

PERSONAL EVALUATION & REFLECTION

Meditate on the following questions and answer them honestly.

1. Do you take care of your body?

2. Do you get the proper rest and exercise? If the answer is no, explain.

3. When is the last time you had a physical examination at your doctor's office?

4. What do you do to maintain a sense of peace in your life?

5. What one thing could you do to improve your self-care?

GROUP DISCUSSION

1. Discuss and answer the question Paul asked in 1 Corinthians 6:19: *"Do you not know that your body is the temple of the Holy Spirit who is in you, whom you have from God, and you are not your own?"*

2. Discuss how a toxic body can lead to a toxic attitude.

3. Discuss the parallel between gluttony and drunkenness. (See Deuteronomy 21:20; Proverbs 23:21.)

4. Discuss gluttony as idolatry as explained in Philippians 3:18–19.

5. Discuss the advantages of spiritually and physically "resting."

GROUP EXERCISE

If someone in the group is struggling in his or her attempt to become healthier, pray for that person.

chapter 21

CONQUERING THE PHILISTINES

OVERCOMING SELF-PITY AND INTIMIDATION

And I will set your bounds from the Red Sea to the sea, Philistia, and from the desert to the River. For I will deliver the inhabitants of the land into your hand, and you shall drive them out before you. (Exodus 23:31)

But if you do not drive out the inhabitants of the land from before you, then it shall be that those whom you let remain shall be irritants in your eyes and thorns in your sides, and they shall harass you in the land where you dwell. (Numbers 33:55)

T he enemy known as the Philistines appears 251 times in the Bible. This is the group David withstood when he killed Goliath. Goliath's threats and intimidation caused Israel to feel inadequate. Instead of fighting, they wallowed in fear and insecurity. (See 1 Samuel 17.) It was also the Philistines with whom Samson tangled when he carried the gates of Gaza to the top of the mount. (See Judges 15.)

This enemy continually showed up in the history of Israel like an infection that would not heal. The word *Philistine* is from the

Hebrew word *plishtiy*. The root of this word is the Hebrew *palash*, which means "to roll in dust" or "wallow oneself." *Palash* is used only three times in Scripture—Jeremiah 6:26; 25:34, and Ezekiel 27:30. Each time it is used, it describes people wallowing in ashes.

> Self-pity will enslave people to the past, blocking their future and potential development.

It's not difficult to understand why God said the Philistines had to be driven out of the land. They used intimidation to gain advantage and left their opponents wallowing in the ashes of defeat.

This helps us understand two things about conquering the Philistines:

1. We must conquer self-pity instead of allowing it to conquer us.

2. We must not give in to intimidation.

FIVE LAWS OF THE PITY PARTY

Law Number One: No One Can Party with Me but Me

The most difficult people to help are those who feel sorry for themselves. Their focus is solely on their *rights* instead of their *responsibilities*. They think they are entitled to certain privileges because of what they have been through and what they did or did not get in life. They feel their misfortune justifies certain needs, wants, and demands from others. In short, they feel they deserve it.

Law Number Two: No One Can Have Anything but Me

Envy and jealousy eat at their hearts until they see nothing but their own needs. They completely lose sight of their blessings, as well as the needs of others. Before they realize it, the characteristic of "never satisfied" matures into the sin of covetousness. They envy what others have in a selfish attempt to reinforce their own feelings of inadequacy. Envy eventually turns to anger, and an insatiable desire for "more things" consumes them.

Law Number Three: No One Can Understand Me but Me

Self-pity eventually enslaves them to the past, blocking their future and potential development. Yesterday's injury becomes today's reason for wrong behavior. Outbursts of anger are justified by "what others have done to me." The disease of "if only" sets in. "If only I had done this; if only I had married this person; if only I had gotten that job." These are the ashes of wallowing in scenes of yesterday. Anyone who questions or challenges their agenda is dismissed as uncaring or misinformed.

Law Number Four: No One Can Encourage Me but Me

The greatest danger of harboring self-pity is that it "justifies" its right to remain. It demands to have more, get more, and do more. As long as you can justify the reason for your self-pity, there is nothing anyone can say to make you feel better. Misery becomes the "cross I must bear."

Law Number Five: No One Can Befriend Me but Me

The cruel companion called "loneliness" moves in and sets up permanent residence with those who feel sorry for themselves. Loneliness wears their clothes, eats at their table, and sings them to sleep at night. The heart hurts, the belly aches, and the pity party continues.

Since the ash pool is only big enough for one at a time, they sit alone and read a sad book with their picture on every page. Anyone who befriends them must wallow too. Their endless stories of yesterday's pain, their extreme views on controversial issues, and their exaggerated version of memories drain their friends emotionally. Too often, the need for closeness is so great that each time someone takes a risk to befriend them, the "emotional vacuum" is set on high as the brave friend is smothered, used up, and discarded.

FIVE LORDS OF THE PHILISTINES

From Sihor, which is east of Egypt, as far as the border of Ekron northward (which is counted as Canaanite); the five lords of the Philistines; the Gazites, the Ashdodites, the Ashkelonites, the Gittites, and the Ekronites; also the Avites. (Joshua 13:3)

A brief resume of the five Philistine kings gives us a snapshot of how intimidation spiritually deports you into a forlorn corner of coward-like conduct.

1. The Gazites

This was Samson's foe. The word *Gazite* means "strong place." The New Testament word for this would be *stronghold*. Paul said, "*The weapons of our warfare are not carnal but mighty in God for pulling down strongholds*" (2 Corinthians 10:4, emphasis added).

> *Too often, their need for closeness is so great that their "emotional vacuum" is set on high, as brave friends are smothered, used up, and discarded.*

A stronghold is a mind-set. It is an intimidating thought that sounds something like this: *You're too fat, too skinny, too ugly, too short, too dumb, too clumsy,* or *too awkward.* This intimidating thought becomes so predominant in our thinking that every other thought has to filter through it. When Samson carried away the gates of Gaza, he was giving us a spiritual illustration that when you tear down the gate, you take out the stronghold.

2. The Ashdodites

The word *Ashdodite* means "I will spoil." Satan uses self-pity to spoil people's lives. He doesn't only want you to think badly of yourself; he also wants to spoil and destroy your life. Satan's plan is to take your birthright from you by attacking your future. He has stirred up the ashes of yesterday so much that you can't see the future because of the dust cloud. Thoughts that create a stronghold in your mind are only decoys.

President John F. Kennedy wrote, "For without belittling the courage with which men have died, we should not forget those acts of courage with which men...have *lived*." Sometimes it takes just as much courage to live as it does to die. When we decide we want our lives back, we are then ready to confront the things that intimidate us.

3. The Ashkelonites

The word *Ashkelonite* is derived from a word meaning "I shall be weighed." Life must be kept in balance. Too much of anything can get your life out of balance. Extremism is a dangerous pattern. All in or all out is not healthy. Intimidation snares with the lie, "If you only had more, you wouldn't feel this way." The key to victory is balance, not more!

4. The Gittites

Goliath was a Gittite. It is derived from the word *Gath*, meaning "winepress." A winepress is a fearful thing to a grape, but it's a beautiful thing to a grape harvester. The press is necessary to make new wine. Satan wants you to think of yourself as the grape. He only wants you to see the hurtful things of life. God, however, wants you to see the overall purpose of your life. Only after we are crushed in His winepress can we fulfill His highest calling. You can either wallow in the ashes of pain or view those same experiences as your sharpener, polishing you for greater service.

Henry Ford said, "Failure is only the opportunity to begin more intelligently." I have never met a great person who did not come through a season of pain. Most great people attribute their inner strength, individuality, and greatness to time spent with pain and disappointment.

5. The Ekronites

Ekronite is derived from the word *Ekron*, meaning "emigration" or "torn up by the roots." Like a group of people who have been forced from their homes, people dealing with self-pity are often unsettled and seem to be searching for something else. An old adage states, "A man with only one watch always knows what time it is. A man with two watches is never quite sure." Choose one thing and stick with it. People who jump from place to place all the time live in a state of confusion.

OUT OF THE ASHES

Most people wallowing in the ashes think they are still in the fire. Usually, the heat went out a long time ago. Their real enemy is not a genuine threat—it is now the *fear* of a threat, which torments them. Intimidation is the real culprit. In the famous words of Franklin D. Roosevelt, "Let me assert my firm belief that the only thing we have to fear is fear itself."

After all, if God is for you, who can be against you? Desperate people don't have to be told to get out of the fire. They get out anyway they can. But when you are wallowing in ashes, you have to choose to get out. Stand up, dust yourself off, and say good-bye to yesterday. Victory is ahead!

Conquering the Philistines

Personal Evaluation & Reflection

Meditate on the following questions and answer them honestly.

1. Do you justify your pity parties or treat them as a dangerous behavioral pattern?

2. Are there any circumstances from your past you have never been able to move beyond? *Test: Do I get angry talking about a particular event in my life? Do I find myself telling the same sad story many times?*

3. Do you suffer from loneliness? Is it justified by circumstances or is it caused by the fact that you feel you can't trust others?

4. What area of your life intimidates you the most? Why?

5. Have you ever considered counseling to help you bring closure to your past hurts?

Group Discussion

1. Discuss the five laws of the pity party.

2. Discuss this sentence: "Since the ash pool is only big enough for one at a time, he or she sits alone and reads a sad book with his or her picture on every page."

3. Discuss the benefits and struggle of life in the winepress.

4. Discuss this quote: "Most people wallowing in the ashes think they are still in the fire. Usually, the heat went out a long time ago."

GROUP EXERCISE

Have the class write a definition for *stronghold*. Now discuss how to pull down a stronghold.

chapter 22

CONQUERING CANAAN

DON'T FORGET THE ORIGINAL VISION

Then I said, "I have labored in vain, I have spent my strength for nothing and in vain; yet surely my just reward is with the LORD, and my work with my God." And now the LORD says, Who formed Me from the womb to be His servant, to bring Jacob back to Him, so that Israel is gathered to Him (for I shall be glorious in the eyes of the LORD, and my God shall be my strength), indeed He says, "It is too small a thing that You should be My servant to raise up the tribes of Jacob, and to restore the preserved ones of Israel; I will also give you as a light to the Gentiles, that you should be My salvation to the ends of the earth."" Thus says the LORD, the Redeemer of Israel, their Holy One, to Him whom man despises, to Him whom the nation abhors, to the Servant of rulers: "Kings shall see and arise, princes also shall worship, because of the LORD who is faithful, the Holy One of Israel; and He has chosen You." Thus says the LORD: "In an acceptable time I have heard You, and in the day of salvation I have helped You; I will preserve You and give You as a covenant to the people, to restore the earth, to cause them to inherit the desolate heritages; that You may say to the prisoners, 'Go forth,' to those who are in darkness, 'Show yourselves.' They shall feed along the roads, and their pastures shall be on all desolate heights. They shall neither hunger nor thirst, neither heat nor sun shall strike them; for He who has mercy on them will lead them, even by the springs of water He will guide them." (Isaiah 49:4–10)

The Lord is raising up deliverers—individuals who have been destined from the womb to make an impact on society. But these heroes may not always look like heroes.

Many of the great moves of God have begun in small rooms on desolate streets with unimportant people. As a matter of fact, God delights in using small beginnings for His glory. It is easy to see how big organizations do big things, but when God decides to do something really big, He usually starts with a humble beginning. He does this for many reasons:

- To make sure the servants will walk by faith and not by sight
- To make sure the great work is bathed in prayer from the beginning
- To make sure He is the foundation
- To ensure the success of the original vision

GOD BEGINS BY PREPARING A PERSON

God raises up the man or woman first before He raises up the ministry.

- Before God could raise up a nation, he had to raise up David.
- Before God could rebuild crumbled Jerusalem, He had to raise up Nehemiah.

- Before God could bring revival to Ninevah, He had to raise up Jonah.

- Before God could set the Israelites free from Egypt's bondage, He had to raise up Moses.

- Before God could bring the Israelites out of captivity under Persia, He had to raise up Esther.

Many of God's people are being raised up for greatness right now, even though it may seem to us that they are struggling. We know what greatness looks like, but do we know what "raising up" looks like?

It looks like hard work and struggle, learning and growing. It's a time of learning to depend totally on God. Sometimes it requires eating the bitter herbs of failure. It is those distasteful times in life, however, that will keep us from the lure of false success, the traps that have entangled others.

> *Many of the great moves of God have begun in small rooms on desolate streets with unimportant people.*

Now, we look for a new breed of victory—victory built on the favor of God. This new breed of warrior is looking for victory that is more personal, more private, and more intimate. A private victory is far more rewarding than a public one.

FINE-TUNING THE ORIGINAL VISION

The original vision is usually the one that lasts the longest. Those who receive a new vision with every new seminar will generally not be the victorious champions. They seek out new ideas so they can be *perceived* to be on the cutting edge, as opposed to seeking out the Cutter of the edge.

God has a plan. To preserve His long-range vision in us, He must bring us to a point of committing to His original vision. To do so, God will give us a vision of the end result. At the time, we may not be able to grasp the fact that it might happen right away, but it also might take years of hard work to get to that vision. We may forget that God showed us our eventual success a few years back. In the small beginnings that we may find ourselves in, things may not look at all like what we envisioned. That's okay.

Fighting Discouragement in the Waiting Room

Sometimes, in the interim between the vision and the victory, we may begin to feel as though all our work is in vain. We begin to accept the status quo, forgetting God's original vision and promise.

That's when God must remind us that His ways are above our ways. He crashes our pity parties and reminds us, "It's not all in vain. Why do you doubt My timing? Don't you know it was I who formed you in your mother's womb?"

Don't Despise Small Things

Zechariah asked the question, *"Who has despised the day of small things?"* (Zechariah 4:10). There is a big difference between starting small and ending small. Most people have struggled to attain what they have. That's the process! Many times things start small. But when God is the foundation, it doesn't matter how large the building gets; it will survive!

In 1886, who would have believed that a seventy-year-old missionary Baptist preacher and a group of Methodist members would start a prayer meeting in a mountain home that would later become the Church of God, which today has millions of members in more than 127 countries around the world? Who would have dreamed in

1906 that a small prayer meeting on Azusa Street under the ministry of W. J. Seymour would become the fountainhead of almost every modern Pentecostal movement in the United States today?

CORNERSTONE ACADEMY

Tammy Walker is a visionary. This talented and gifted teacher dreamed of having her own school. She was certainly not looking for work, having already been the principal of one of the finest and largest Christian schools in St. Louis. Her reputation for quality and excellence preceded her and ranked her among the top in her field in metropolitan St. Louis.

When God is the foundation, it doesn't matter how large the building gets; it will survive!

After teaching college for a while, Tammy decided to work with children who had special needs. At first it seemed to bring her closer to her goal of nurturing, protecting, and loving children. But deep inside she had a longing to lead a unique school of her own. Her goals seemed impossible to reach, even though her family and close friends surrounded her with support.

The first leap of faith came when she hired her staff. The fledgling school could not guarantee steady paychecks. To push her even further out on a limb, Cornerstone Christian Academy was birthed out of Twin Rivers Worship Center, the church where I pastor. It was during the heat of our building construction. Therefore, the school had no sign, no playground, no normal entranceway, no guaranteed schedule; yet they possessed a vision.

Two weeks before classes were to begin, there was no drywall in the classrooms, no drop ceilings—only exposed beams and wires.

Yet Tammy put on her best smile and walked prospective parents through the construction, sharing her vision and painting word pictures as she gave her tours. To some, Tammy just had a creative imagination. To others she had faith.

While a few caught Tammy's vision, she soon learned that the walk of faith is sometimes a lonely one. She and her little troop of dedicated teachers rolled up their sleeves and made the best of things. Because of the lack of funds, she became the principal, the janitor, and a teacher—all for no pay. Those were stressful days, but as the result of her faith, vision, and trust in God, Cornerstone Christian Academy was born.

One year later, the school quadrupled in size and added two more grades. Today it is one of the fastest growing and most widely respected Christian schools in metropolitan St. Louis.

LITTLE IS MUCH WHEN GOD IS IN IT

When God is working in our lives, what we do may cause a ripple that will affect kings, princes, and rulers. Who would have believed that...

- a baby placed in the bulrushes would be used to deliver three million slaves?

- a Baby born in a manger to a teenaged virgin girl would rewrite history?

- Jesus would turn the world upside down by discipling only twelve men in three and a half short years?

- the Gospel would spread in Samaria because of one woman whom Jesus met at a well?

- one hundred twenty people in an upper room would be the beginning of Pentecost?

- Martin Luther nailing his 95 theses document to the door of Castle Church in Wittenburg would spark the beginning of what is now referred to as the Protestant Reformation?

- a boys' club at Oxford University would be the beginning of the great Methodist denomination?

- a revival that was considered unsuccessful because only one young boy was saved would produce the ministry of international evangelist Billy Graham?

THE DAY OF SALVATION

God is preparing you for ministry so that you can change society and rewrite history. God may be raising you up for a season of greatness, and from that season will flow a fountain of blessings that will reach future generations. The original vision will always sound something like Isaiah 49:8–10:

> *Thus says the LORD: "In an acceptable time I have heard You, and in the day of salvation I have helped You; I will preserve You and give You as a covenant to the people, to restore the earth, to cause them to inherit the desolate heritages; that You may say to the prisoners, 'Go forth,' to those who are in darkness, 'Show yourselves.' They shall feed along the roads, and their pastures shall be on all desolate heights. They shall neither hunger nor thirst, neither heat nor sun shall strike them; for He who has mercy on them will lead them, even by the springs of water He will guide them.*

Setting captives free, healing broken hearts, evangelizing the lost—this is usually how the original vision begins. But many times when we see God's favor and the numbers increase, we try to change the vision.

Some people can't handle success. They forget where they came from and who brought them there. When growth gets their eyes on themselves instead of their original vision, many will exchange deliverance for popularity, salvation for stardom, and power for politics.

YOU ALREADY HAVE THE ANSWER

Habakkuk 2:2 says, *"Then the LORD answered me and said: 'Write the vision and make it plain on tablets, that he may run who reads it.'"*

The key to success lies within the first vision God gives you. Writing down your original vision is the key to fulfilling it. Yet we shouldn't just write it down; we should give it away so others will be inspired, as well. Our purpose, direction, and plan are already there. Instead of looking for new insight, simply getting in touch with the original vision can jumpstart our progress. We already have the answer. The same thing that brought us this far with God will take us the rest of the way—if we follow His original vision.

When God gives you a vision, write it down! Then, whatever you do, however big you become, by all means, stay the course!

CONQUERING CANAAN

PERSONAL EVALUATION & REFLECTION

Meditate on the following questions and answer them honestly.

1. Can you see how God has prepared you in times past for present-day ministry?

2. What area of your life is God working on right now?

3. What do you feel God has raised up you to do?

4. Have you ever written your testimony? If not, take the time to write it now.

5. What are some of the things that have caused you to detour from your original vision?

GROUP DISCUSSION

1. Discuss God's process of God raising up the minister before He raises up the ministry.

2. Discuss the Scripture in Zechariah 4:10, *"Who has despised the day of small things?"*

3. Discuss the original vision of your church or ministry.

   • What was the motivating factor for birthing it into existence?

   • Is that still the goal today?

- Is the goal being accomplished?

4. Does your church or ministry have its vision in writing? Is it plain? Read Habakkuk 2:2 and discuss the importance of this instruction in becoming victorious.

5. Discuss the interval between the vision and the victory.

GROUP EXERCISE

1. Ask members of the class to share testimonies about God's process in raising them up for ministry.

2. Ask members of the group to discuss unfulfilled prophecy that still awaits fruition in their lives, or unfulfilled visions that are still coming to pass.

ABOUT THE AUTHOR

Bryan Cutshall is the senior pastor of Twin Rivers Worship Center in St. Louis, Missouri. As a long-term pastor, he watched Twin Rivers church grow from fifty-two people to one of the most vital megachurches in the Midwest.

Bryan is a pastor, convention speaker, and church trainer. Each year he trains thousands of church leaders in conferences and diagnostic clinics. He is the author of several books, as well as the creator of the "Church Trainer" label, which is a resource line for training pastors, leaders, and Christian workers. All of his books and resources can be found at www.churchtrainer.com.

He and his wife, Faith, have two daughters, Brittany and Lindsay.

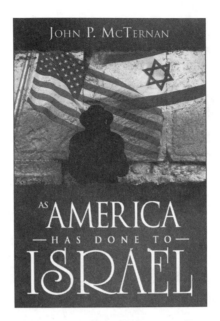

As America Has Done to Israel

John McTernan

God's everlasting promise to bless those who bless Israel—and curse those who curse Israel—is still in effect today. Throughout its history, America has been in a unique position to bless the Jewish people and has experienced many blessings as a result. In more recent years, however, America has failed to consistently stand by Israel and suffered dramatic disasters. In this thought-provoking book, John McTernan traces how America's spectacular rise to power was tied to blessing the Jews. He also examines the times when America defaulted on this call—and the dire consequences that followed. Torn from today's headlines, *As America Has Done to Israel* is a must-read for all Christians who love God, love their country, and desire to walk in His ways!

ISBN: 978-1-60374-038-8 • Trade • 304 pages

www.whitakerhouse.com

Gateway to God's Blessing
Derek Prince

The Bible says that the fear of the Lord is the *"beginning of wisdom"* (Psalm 111:10) and the *"beginning of knowledge"* (Proverbs 1:7). Proverbs 14:27 even calls it a *"fountain of life"*! But do people really understand what is meant by *"the fear of the Lᴏʀᴅ"*? Drastically different from the frightful trembling we feel in response to a threatening person or dangerous situation, the fear of the Lord is a deep sense of reverence and awe of the One who created us, loves us, and saved us. With comforting words of instruction, Bible scholar Derek Prince explains how to gain wisdom and understanding that are rooted in the fear of the Lord, how to overcome pride in order to submit to Christ and to others, and how to stand in awe of God's holiness. Experience peace and confidence by cultivating the fear of the Lord, the *Gateway to God's Blessing*!

ISBN: 978-1-60374-052-4 • Trade • 176 pages

www.whitakerhouse.com

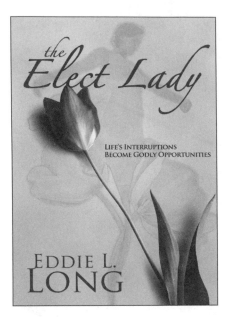

The Elect Lady:
Life's Interruptions Become Godly Opportunites
Eddie L. Long

Growing up, most little girls dream of loving husbands, beautiful homes, and perfect children. What happens when life doesn't turn out the way they expected?

To all the women who wonder what went wrong in their lives, Bishop Eddie Long brings this powerful message: Elect Lady, God sees your circumstances. The path to which He has called you may not be easy, but you are in the position to influence your children, your neighborhood, your church, and the world. *The Elect Lady*, a life-changing book written from the depths of Eddie Long's heart, will help you to receive God's best for your life, turn past mistakes into triumphs, recognize God's interruptions in your life as His divine direction, and discover that He has a better plan for you than you can imagine for yourself.

ISBN: 978-0-88368-281-4 • Hardcover • 192 pages

WHITAKER
HOUSE

www.whitakerhouse.com

Authority Abusers:
Toxic Leadership and Its Effects in Homes, Churches, and Relationships
(revised and expanded edition)
George G. Bloomer

As surely as the absence of authority produces chaos, the abuse of authority produces destruction. Tragically, it's inside the church—where salvation and love should abound—that some of the worst authority abuse takes place. God's design for authority has been misunderstood, twisted, and manipulated, leaving innocent people as victims and prisoners of controlling, abusive situations.

Wake up! This is not God's design for the church— or authority.

In this newly revised and expanded edition of *Authority Abusers*, Bishop George Bloomer shows you the key to breaking free from the bondage of spiritual abuse.

ISBN: 978-1-60374-046-3 • Hardcover • 208 pages

WHITAKER
HOUSE

www.whitakerhouse.com

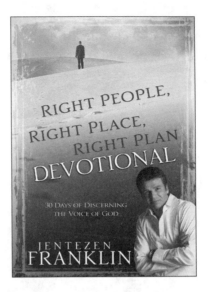

Right People, Right Place, Right Plan Devotional:
30 Days of Discerning the Voice of God
Jentezen Franklin

In this thirty-day journey of discerning the voice of God, Jentezen Franklin focuses on the three central elements of his best-selling book, *Right People, Right Place, Right Plan*. Discover the importance of associating with the right people, being in the right place, and having the right plan, and learn to listen to God's voice and to respond to life's circumstances with insight and unwavering faith through these life-changing daily meditations.

God has bestowed the incredible gift of discernment into the heart of every believer. He has given you an internal compass to help guide your family, your finances, and every other aspect of your life. Join Jentezen Franklin as he reveals how you can tap into your supernatural gift of spiritual discernment to fulfill your purpose as a child of God.

ISBN: 978-1-60374-059-3 • Gift Book, Hardcover • 144 pages

WHITAKER
HOUSE

www.whitakerhouse.com